Lifelong Learning

Andrew Holmes

- Fast track route to increasing your intellectual capital by mastering all aspects of lifelong learning

- Covers all the key techniques of lifelong learning, from keeping a learning log and a self-development plan to finding a personal coach/mentor and getting yourself published

- Examples and lessons from successful companies that generate a continuous learning culture including Barclays and The Leverage Organisation, and ideas from the smartest thinkers in the field

- Includes a glossary of key concepts and a comprehensive resources guide

LIFE & WORK

10.06

essential management thinking at your fingertips

The right of Andrew Holmes to be identified as the author of this work has been asserted in accordance with the Copyright, Designs and Patents Act 1988

First published 2002 by
Capstone Publishing (A Wiley Company)
8 Newtec Place
Magdalen Road
Oxford OX4 1RE
United Kingdom
http://www.capstoneideas.com

CIP catalogue records for this book are available from the British Library and the US Library of Congress

ISBN 1-84112-257-2

Printed and bound in Great Britain by CPI Antony Rowe, Eastbourne

This book is printed on acid-free paper

Substantial discounts on bulk quantities of Capstone books are available to corporations, professional associations and other organizations. Please contact Capstone for more details on +44 (0)1865 798 623 or (fax) +44 (0)1865 240 941 or (e-mail) info@wiley-capstone.co.uk

Contents

Introduction to ExpressExec

ExpressExec is 3 million words of the latest management thinking compiled into 10 modules. Each module contains 10 individual titles forming a comprehensive resource of current business practice written by leading practitioners in their field. From brand management to balanced scorecard, ExpressExec enables you to grasp the key concepts behind each subject and implement the theory immediately. Each of the 100 titles is available in print and electronic formats.

Through the ExpressExec.com Website you will discover that you can access the complete resource in a number of ways:

» printed books or e-books;
» e-content – PDF or XML (for licensed syndication) adding value to an intranet or Internet site;
» a corporate e-learning/knowledge management solution providing a cost-effective platform for developing skills and sharing knowledge within an organization;
» bespoke delivery – tailored solutions to solve your need.

Why not visit www.expressexec.com and register for free key management briefings, a monthly newsletter and interactive skills checklists. Share your ideas about ExpressExec and your thoughts about business today.

Please contact elound@wiley-capstone.co.uk for more information.

Introduction to Lifelong Learning

Why is lifelong learning such an issue? This chapter considers the changing nature of working life and knowledge, including:

» how the half-life of knowledge is reducing;
» how globalization and technology are changing the nature of work;
» how organizations are responding; and
» why we must all embrace lifelong learning.

"In a time of drastic change it is the learners who inherit the future. The learned usually find themselves equipped to live in a world that no longer exists."

Eric Hoffer, philosopher.

Consider the following.

» Our working lives are increasingly defined by what we know rather than who we work for, our position, status or title.
» The explosive growth of data is leading to information overload and an inability to maintain a sense of control over our working and non-working lives. Individuals now retain less than 20 per cent of the knowledge they require to be effective in their jobs. Compare this to the 70 per cent they were able to retain in the 1990s.[1]
» A job for life can no longer be guaranteed by any employer, indeed working life for the white-collar worker increasingly resembles an industrial age sweatshop.
» Average job tenure in United States firms has fallen from 23 years between 1950 and 1960 to 2–2.5 years today, and the average worker will have five different employers during the course of their career.
» Globalization is forcing organizations to routinely redefine the skills and competencies of their employees, and it is now much easier for them to develop and deliver products and services using cheaper labor available elsewhere in the world. Increasingly developing countries are able to compete with the industrialized world with very well educated people at a significantly reduced cost.
» The majority of employees receive between five and ten days training per year, but with the half-life of knowledge getting shorter, we have to ask if it is enough. The stock of human knowledge now doubles every five years, and by 2020 it is expected to double every 73 days.[2]
» Most people leave their firms to develop skills rather than earn more money. And, replacing a manager/professional costs companies 18 months' salary.[3]

The last decades of the twentieth century witnessed unprecedented change across the industrialized world. The increasingly wired world that stimulated the globalization of commerce brought with it new challenges for governments, organizations but especially individuals.

No longer sheltered from the vagaries of economic downturn overseas, individuals have been subject to the rapid and brutal swings of the global economy. For many people this has resulted in them being "downsized" as major corporations cut their headcounts to improve profitability and competitiveness. But as well as such coarse changes, there are more subtle ones that arise from the impacts of technology and its ability to displace employment. All serve to reduce the shelf life of the average employee who, although equipped for today, is rarely equipped for tomorrow. What is more worrying is that the majority of us are unprepared for such changes. Preparing for the changes ahead requires us to become much more adaptable and willing to learn continuously.

Learning begins (or fails to begin) within the family setting. During our early childhood we are heavily influenced by our parents as they encourage the exploration of new ideas within a safe and risk free environment. At this stage of our development we absorb huge amounts of information. Our formal learning begins once we enter nursery school and continues through primary, secondary, and for an increasing number of people, tertiary institutions. The impact of this formal learning process should not be underestimated. The Organization for Economic Co-operation and Development (OECD) found that better educated people are more likely to be in work and less likely to be unemployed.[4] Despite the essential foundations that the formal education and learning process provides, learning often takes a back seat once we enter the workplace. And for some it stops altogether, either because learning seems to have lost its importance, or because they have been turned off by 10–15 years' hard slog in the classroom. Instead we become defined by our work and the need to hold down our jobs, pay our bills, bring up children and cope with the rigors of working life.

Within the work setting learning becomes restricted to understanding the bare essentials of a particular process, system or operational function. Therefore, learning, when it takes place, is work-based and narrowly focused. Life becomes routine: a succession of events not much different from the last. We all get comfortable working for the same employer, executing the same tasks and spending time with the same people. But given the impacts of technological change and globalization, this type of existence is increasingly tenuous. As the rate of change increases, our ability to cope with it reduces because we are unused to learning, unlearning and relearning. It is no wonder then that workers are more stressed than ever before, feel out of control and are generally fearful of the future. But at the same time, we hear of skill shortages, graduates who are poorly prepared for the modern workplace, and the need to reinvent ourselves through continuous learning.

The real challenge, therefore, is the upgrading and transformation of our skills to maintain our employability well into the future. People with outdated vocational skills will find it increasingly difficult to maintain their levels of income, or in some cases, any income at all. Indeed we are already witnessing the gradual decline in benefits, pay and quality of work for a large proportion of white-collar workers in the United States. Only those at the high-end of the knowledge economy seem to be increasing their prospects. The people most at risk are those of us who are some 10, 20 or 30 years into our careers because most training and retraining is geared to the young, not the mid-career professional. It is clear that new jobs demanding old skills will not materialize; new jobs require new skills. With governments and organizations generally slow to respond to these issues, it is up to the individual to ensure they are appropriately skilled throughout their careers.

The good news is that it is possible to respond by developing the mental adaptability we naturally had as children and honed during our formal education. Learning, unlearning and relearning does not have to be a chore, and the economic benefits to the individual can be significant. Moreover, lifelong learning is the key to longevity within the workplace and the essential foundation of the learning organization. Those that develop the ability to continuously learn will inherit the organization of the future. In doing so they will be able to adapt more readily to the changing business environment and maintain their upward careers.

This resource reviews the key elements of lifelong learning (Chapter 2), describes its evolution (Chapter 3), describes the electronic and global dimensions (Chapters 4 and 5) and provides the busy executive with all they need to know about lifelong learning and how to make it work for themselves and their organization.

NOTES

1. Hill, D. (2001) "Keep it Simple." *People Performance*, (June), pp. 42–3.
2. DTI (2001) *The Future of Corporate Learning*. Department of Trade & Industry Report, London, p. 6–.
3. Donkin, R. (2001) "A fresh dawn for the talent market: Technology and demographic change are combining to give the individual an edge over the unimaginative employer." *Financial Times*, May 3.
4. OECD (2001) *The Well-Being of Nations: The Role of Human and Social Capital*. Organisation for Economic Cooperation & Development, Paris, p. 28.

What is Lifelong Learning?

Most people confuse training with lifelong learning, and many do not understand what forms lifelong learning can take. This chapter therefore covers some of the basics, including:

» defining training, learning and lifelong learning;
» outlining the role of the organization in lifelong learning;
» identifying the various forms which lifelong learning can take;
» showing who benefits from lifelong learning; and
» describing how to be successful at lifelong learning.

"Learning is the process of individuals constructing and transforming experience into knowledge, skills, attitudes, values, beliefs, emotions ... "

Peter Jarvis, Professor of Continuing Education, University of
Surrey.

"All purposeful learning activity, whether formal or informal, is undertaken on an ongoing basis with the aim of improving knowledge, skills and competence."

Organisation for Economic Cooperation & Development.

The term lifelong learning originated approximately ten years ago within the OECD, which was seeking to place emphasis on outputs (learning) rather than inputs (education, training and self study). But before we say what lifelong learning is, it is necessary to say what it isn't.

WHAT LIFELONG LEARNING ISN'T

Lifelong learning is not just another name for training. Although an essential part of our development, training conjures up a restrictive view of the learning process. Martyn Sloman, author of *The E-learning Revolution*, offers a useful definition of both, which draws out the key differences between the two.

"Training – the process of acquiring the knowledge and skills related to work requirements using formal, structured or guided means, but excluding general supervision, job-specific innovations and learning by experience ... Training lies within the domain of organization: it is an intervention designed to produce behaviors from individuals that have positive organizational results."

"Learning – the physical and mental process involved in changing one's normal behavioral patterns and habits... Learning lies within the domain of the individual, can result from a whole range of experiences, and can be positive, negative or neutral from the organization's point of view."

By the same token, lifelong learning is not about continuing professional development (CPD). CPD is an increasingly important aspect to a professional's life. For some failing to maintain their CPD can result in expulsion from their profession. But the key point about CPD is that it is imposed by the professional institution. As a result only a small percentage of professionals take up the CPD programs on offer. According to one review, only 10–20 per cent ever take part.[1] And just as with training, this can be a somewhat passive exercise, with limited learning value. For example, it is possible to class the attendance at a conference as CPD, but one could attend and learn nothing. Keeping a log of such activities merely indicates that you have attended. It does not necessarily mean you have learnt something. Because the profession drives CPD, it is not sufficiently focused on the individual.

There has also been some debate and confusion about lifelong learning. Eddy Knasel, John Meed and Anna Rossetti in their book *Learn for Your Life*, help to clear up some of the confusion by making the distinction between career, lifelong and life-wide learning.

» Career learning is often directly associated with work, careers and their management.
» Life-wide/lifetime learning is the term most often used by policy makers to describe the provision of education and training for people throughout their working lives.
» Lifelong learning is learning that occurs throughout a person's life.

WHAT LIFELONG LEARNING IS

Although lifelong learning is not restricted to the workplace for the purposes of this resource, I define lifelong learning as both an attitude and a discipline that extends beyond vocational and work-focused on-the-job training, and which encapsulates the soft skills such as interpersonal communication, teamwork, emotional intelligence and problem solving. Lifelong learning is principally focused on maintaining longevity within one's working life, and is controlled by the individual, not the organization.

This definition is more akin to life-wide and lifetime learning, but goes wider by placing responsibility on the individual. Ultimately, for those in work, lifelong learning will always take on a work focus. Thus, learning in this context is a means to an end, rather than an end itself.

We will learn more about the reasons why lifelong learning is such a critical issue in Chapter 3.

THE ROLE OF THE ORGANIZATION

Any discussion of lifelong learning and its importance to our careers would be incomplete without a mention of the organization's role in making it happen. Although lifelong learning starts and ends with the individual, organizations must create an environment that promotes it, especially if they wish to become learning organizations themselves. To do so requires commitment from the board, which itself must become what Bob Garrett in his book, *The Fish Rots From the Head*, terms the learning board. After all, if the board fails to learn, it is unlikely that the rest of the organization will learn either. Garrett reinforces this point, by introducing four preconditions for this to work.

» Everyone in the organization has to be encouraged to learn from their daily work and, more importantly, time must be set aside to do so.
» Systems and processes must be in place that can capture learning, share it, celebrate and use it.
» The organization as a whole should be encouraged to transform itself through its internal and external learning processes.
» Learning should be valued in the appraisal process and included within people's compensation.

Organizations are still caught up within the knowledge revolution and have busied themselves creating knowledge managers, coordinators and facilitators as well as the processes and technical infrastructures for its management. Knowledge is, of course, an essential building block to learning and the creation of the learning organization.

THE MANY FORMS OF LIFELONG LEARNING

Because lifelong learning is an inherently personal affair, there is no single model on which to base individual learning. However, we should all recognize that learning can be planned as well as accidental and this therefore requires us to be sufficiently sensitive and open minded to the learning opportunities around us. The opportunity to learn falls into the following broad categories.

» Personal development – the way we as individuals develop our inter-personal and intra-personal skills and capabilities.
» Planned development – following formal courses, such as degrees, MBAs, technical qualifications and so on. This also includes the various forms of training received during our working lives.
» Accidental development – unplanned learning that occurs during the course of our working and non-working lives.
» Experience-based development – learning by doing. This would include advancing skills and abilities through practice as well as learning new ones by observing others who have them.

Unwrapping this further suggests we can learn from a variety of sources, including the following.

» Customers – often the only way we find out about our products and services.
» Colleagues – a great source of insight and one of the few ways to articulate much of the tacit knowledge that exists in most organiza-tions.
» Success – there is always the danger that success breeds arrogance. But success does provide a golden opportunity to develop an under-standing of how and why it came about and use this to model the process through which it was achieved. Modeling success is one of the key themes within neuro-linguistic programming, which is described in Chapter 8.
» Failure – although always painful, failures provide the perfect ground for learning as long as we have the stomach to do so.
» Books – obvious to state, and yet only a small minority bother.
» Daily routines – experience is one of the most effective ways of learning anything new, and our daily routine is often a relatively safe environment within which to test new ideas.
» Projects – if you are fortunate enough to be involved with projects, they are a perfect way to learn about the corporation, innovation and politics.

As we will see throughout this resource, if lifelong learning is to provide the benefits we seek, it must be broad based and encapsulate the following.

» Technical learning – required to fulfill day-to-day responsibilities.

» Emotional learning – associated with our ability to cope with different personalities, situations and challenges.
» Intellectual learning – associated with broadening our general understanding of the environment around us (including work) in order to develop lateral thinking skills.
» Interpersonal and intra-personal learning – necessary to both understand ourselves as well as others.
» Cultural learning – as commerce goes global, our ability to work within complex, global organizations and across different regions around the world requires us to learn more about other cultures. You can learn more about the issues of globalization and lifelong learning in Chapter 5.
» Political learning – an increasingly important ability within the workplace, and yet so many people shy away from it. The only advice here is, ignore it at your peril.

WHO BENEFITS FROM LIFELONG LEARNING?

Lifelong learning has the capability of benefiting all parties involved in the process.

» Individuals benefit from increased career choices, employability and the potential of increased earnings. The adage, "the more you learn, the more you earn" holds true.
» Employers benefit from the increased flexibility that comes from a well-educated workforce and this translates to a healthy bottom line. For example, companies that invest in learning typically outperform the market by 45 per cent, whilst companies that don't, under perform by 22 per cent. They also benefit from higher retention rates, which, again, reduces their costs, especially given that the average cost of losing an employee is $50,000. For example, only 12 per cent of employees plan to leave an employer that offers excellent training opportunities. Compare that to the 41 per cent who plan to leave those that offer poor levels and quality of training.[2]
» The state/nation benefits from a general increase in the skills of its population, which filters into an enhanced gross domestic product and competitive global position, as well as increased inward investment and tax take from high earners.

BEING SUCCESSFUL AT LIFELONG LEARNING

According to Alastair Rylatt, author of *Learning Unlimited*, a commitment to learning requires a commitment to other things, including a desire to make a difference, being open to discovery of new options, taking risks and being tolerant to the uncertainty of modern times. The chapters in this resource will provide you with sufficient information on which to make up your own mind. And for those who are willing to take up the challenge, 10 steps to success have been included in Chapter 10.

But success in lifelong learning requires more than a commitment to learn, it also requires a commitment to unlearn and forget those things we know that are no longer relevant or which are preventing us from accepting new ideas. Look at Microsoft, for example. Back in 1995, Bill Gates dismissed the Internet as an irrelevance, and yet a few years later, when the significance of the Internet was clear, he was able to mobilize his entire organization to take on and win at the Internet. This required unlearning entrenched views of what the Internet meant, and new concepts learnt and applied. As John Maynard Keynes the pre-eminent economist said, ''The greatest difficulty in the world is not for people to accept new ideas, but to make them forget about old ideas.''

KEY LEARNING POINTS
- » Lifelong learning is not the same thing as training.
- » Lifelong learning is an attitude and ethos rather than a process.
- » For most people lifelong learning is career-focused learning which has technical, and non-technical elements.
- » The success of the learning organization depends on everyone's ability to learn. This includes the board of directors.
- » Most organizations are still in the era of knowledge and knowledge management.
- » Learning can be accidental as well as planned.
- » If we are to maintain our careers, lifelong learning must be very broad.
- » The greatest challenge in lifelong learning is not learning but unlearning.

NOTES

1. Hemmington, N. (1999) "Creating a culture of life-long learning at work." *Continuing Professional Development*, Issue 3.
2. See www.saba.com/about.

The Evolution of Lifelong Learning

The impacts of technological change and globalization lie at the heart of lifelong learning, but how has it evolved? This chapter examines:

» the rise of the knowledge worker;
» the implications of the globalization of commerce;
» the ageing of the population and its impact on employment;
» the increasing insecurity of working life; and
» the rise of the white collar sweatshop.

"... knowledge workers need to be educated in abstract thinking, system thinking, experimentation and collaboration..."

R. Reich, management writer.

"The whole game is moving to a higher level. So there is a growing premium on people, at all ends of the skill spectrum, who can work smarter, faster and better. You want people to be innovative (within guidelines) passionate (within reason), and armed with sufficient discretion to make mistakes (as long as they are not too big). Demand for those people is going to outpace supply for the foreseeable future."

Bruce Tulgan, management writer and founder of
Rainmaking Thinking.

Lifelong learning is a recent phenomenon but one that is beginning to enter the consciousness of governments, organizations and individuals. Its roots lie in the increasing vulnerability of organizations and their workforces, to the subtle (and not so subtle) effects of technological change, globalization and population ageing. The following paragraphs trace its origins.

THE RISE OF THE KNOWLEDGE WORKER, 1900–1980

For literally millennia our very survival depended upon our ability to work the land. Physical toil was the mainstay of the population. During this time, power resided in those that owned the land, rather than those that toiled upon it. It was only in the aftermath of the Black Death during the fourteenth century, which killed at least a third of Europe's population, that landlords found the balance of power had shifted to those serfs still alive and capable of work.

However, the truly momentous changes occurred with the Agricultural Revolution of the eighteenth century and the Industrial Revolution of the nineteenth century, which began to establish the beginnings of the knowledge worker. Although the majority of people still worked the land, an increasing number worked in factories, and with machinery that needed tending and maintenance. This required specialist skills, rather than the brute strength that typified the past. It also necessitated changes in the nature of work and required workers to update their skills to remain in employment. As to be expected in times of great change, those without the requisite skills or adaptability found themselves out of work. In some cases they reacted violently, as with the anti-factory Luddite movement in England. Power resided in the factory owners and their financial backers, rather than those that sweated in the factories.

But, it was the emergence of the computer during the 1950s that unleashed the current shift in work patterns, the heralding of the information age and the increasing dependence on knowledge and a knowledgeable workforce. A look at the United States' Census Bureau data between 1900 and 1980 illustrates the changes in the distribution of work very well. During this period, the percentage of farm workers as a proportion of the total workforce fell from 37.5 per cent in 1900 to 2.8 per cent in 1980. Over this same period, the percentage involved with manual and service work remained fairly static at around 45 per cent. But white-collar work grew from 17.6 to 52.2 per cent over these 80 years.[1] These days our well-being depends less on what we can do, and more on what we know. Harnessing our intellectual capital is thus the key to success in an ever-complex workplace.

THE GLOBALIZATION OF COMMERCE, 1960–2000

The process of globalization started during the 1960s with the emergence of multinational and transnational corporations that coincided with the expansion of international trade following the Second World War. During the 1970s a number of factors came together that molded globalization into what we know today. These factors included the following.[2]

» The internationalizing of capital markets.
» The expansion of international securities investment and bank lending.
» The increasing sophistication of information technology used within commerce.
» The emergence of the Internet.
» Economic competition from Japan.

» The General Agreement on Tariffs and Trade of 1947.
» The reduction in state control and the subsequent rise in deregulation.
» The oil crisis.

Each of these factors led governments and organizations to consider how they could remain competitive in a commercial environment with fewer controls and increased competition. Many corporations responded by merging with, or acquiring other organizations that were better placed to deliver a truly global service. Others sought out the cheapest labor with which to manufacture their goods, leading to a massive reduction in the manufacturing bases of the industrialized world as the work was transferred to the cheaper economies of the Far East, Central Asia and, more recently, China.

With further advances in technology since the 1970s, globalization is increasingly allowing the transfer of knowledge around the world. And, with the emerging economies of Asia providing a ready source of well-educated cheap labor, corporations are beginning to source their knowledge workers overseas rather than at home. In addition, as the competition hots up, corporations are having to develop more sophisticated knowledge-based products and services in order to compete within the global market. The process of globalization is therefore leading to an increase in the levels of uncertainty for us all, as it causes corporations to reconsider their hiring, location, and skill needs far more regularly than in the past. It is also leading to an upsurge in the demand for smart, versatile employees who are capable of learning, unlearning and relearning.

THE END OF THE BABY BOOM

The populations of the industrialized world are growing older. The sons and daughters of the 1960s baby boom and the secondary boom that began in the mid-1970s and peaked in 1990 are hurtling towards middle age and retirement. This is introducing significant downside risks on corporations and nations around the world. For example, the proportion of the United Kingdom's population aged under 18 will fall from 7 to 6.6 million between now and 2011. At the same time the proportion aged 60 and over will increase from 12.1 to 14 million.[3]

Japan has already reached an average age of over 40 and its population is expected to decline after peaking in 2007.[4]

Companies, it seems, can no longer rely on a stream of fresh-faced twenty-something recruits to add to their existing pool of workers. Couple this with an aging workforce, and there are major problems on the horizon for organizations and workers alike. It is well known that it is harder to change an older workforce than a younger, more adaptable one. Paul Wallace, author of *Agequake*, draws a parallel with industrial plants: "New recruits are rather like greenfield sites – capable of much more efficient production to meet today's industrial needs – while older workers are more like long-established plants, difficult to adapt to new working practices." This poses problems for us all. Organizations will have to respond by a combination of:

» reconsidering the way they train staff, as they grow older;
» transferring their operations to the younger nations of the world; and
» tempting employees from overseas through immigration (such as the United Kingdom is doing to reduce shortfalls in teachers and nurses).

Employees (you and me) will have to get very good at changing and learning – or face a depressing future of limited employment opportunities, and short-term contracts.

THE BEGINNINGS OF WHITE-COLLAR INSECURITY

Previous "revolutions" such as the Industrial Revolution only affected those whose livelihood depended upon their physical prowess. The coming of the Information Age changed all this and ensured the revolution was felt much wider than ever before. With the advance of the computer, white-collar workers, whose intellectual abilities had been safe from the previous disruptions in the job market, started to feel the cold wind of change. Great tranches of white-collar jobs were eradicated during the early years of computerization as computers replaced basic financial processes.

As the process of automation continued, the level of uncertainty about longevity in the workplace increased. But it was the emergence of business process re-engineering (BPR) during the 1990s that led to the most significant changes. BPR was designed to achieve the long awaited benefits from technology and make the corporation, with fewer employees, more effective and efficient. Initially starting within the manufacturing sector, it soon spread into the service, utilities and public sectors with dramatic effects. It wasn't long before business process re-engineering became synonymous with downsizing. During the 1990s millions of workers were downsized as the wave of headcount reductions swept the United States, the United Kingdom and Europe.

And with it came the massive insecurities of the modern workplace. More worryingly, it led to the destruction of the psychological contract between employee and employer and the dawning realization that a single job for life with regular promotions was no longer a viable option. A person's working life was no longer framed by a single organization, nor did it depend on who they knew. Instead it depended on their usefulness to the organization, what they knew, their ability to change, and so on. Thus white-collar workers everywhere started to realize that knowledge was power and the ability to capture it and use it was their ticket to long-term employability.

THE EMERGENCE OF THE WHITE-COLLAR SWEATSHOP

Over the last decade the quality of white-collar work has gradually deteriorated for the majority of employees. The combined effect of technological change and globalization has resulted in an intensification of work. Jill Andresky Fraser in her book *White-Collar Sweatshop*[5] identifies five issues that face us all in our working lives.

» Increasing hours – Americans are working longer and harder – 25 million now work more than 49 hours a week, with a large number working a lot more; 11 million spend 60 hours or more at work.
» Job spill – an increasing amount of work is conducted outside of traditional working hours, mainly at home. Thus work spills over to leisure time and invades family life. Some 39 per cent of Americans no longer take lunch breaks. In addition, commuting "dead time" is becoming an extension of the working day, made possible by cellular phones, laptops and wireless links to the office.

» Less time to unwind – with work spilling over to weekends and evenings, white-collar workers are finding themselves squeezed, with little or no time to unwind and recover from the working day. Worse still is that vacations too are being reduced through cost cutting initiatives, reducing even further the time to recharge.

» Too much stress – despite the impacts of job spill, longer hours and reduced time to unwind, Americans are finding it ever more difficult to keep up with demanding schedules. According to the American Management Association, almost 50 per cent of Americans now feel stressed at work. Stress is a way of life for many white-collar workers irrespective of age or position within the corporate hierarchy. This stress is in part driven by the fear of losing their jobs if they are not seen to be keeping up.

» At the same time as expecting more from their employees, employers are scaling back the rewards they provide – for example, middle-income families in America saw their income rise by just $780 between 1988 and 1998. Moreover, companies are employing an increasing number of contingent and part-time workers who find it very difficult to move into full-time employment.

SO WHY BOTHER WITH LIFELONG LEARNING?

What can we conclude from all of the changes outlined above, especially in relation to lifelong learning?

» We must recognize that the ability to learn is an essential skill we all need if we are to cope with and survive the demands of the modern workplace. Charles Handy's prediction of portfolio work and its significance to us all, if not already here for many, is on the horizon for us all. Organizations in the future will need people who are ready, willing and able to learn and change. And given that 50 per cent of all employees' skills become outdated within 3–5 years, the necessity to learn cannot be overstated.

» Learning must extend beyond the obvious functional and technical skills and disciplines we have been used to developing. Knowledge work depends on other skills that are more socially based. Increasingly, therefore, we will have to learn coping, influencing and emotional skills so that we can work smarter rather than just harder. As we saw in Chapter 2, learning should not be confused with training.

» Corporations are realizing that their very survival depends upon the skills, competencies and attitudes of their employees and more importantly, their ability to learn. Many are taking steps to help their workforces to learn. More will be said about how corporations are stimulating lifelong learning in Chapters 6 and 7.

» Policy makers are waking up to the knowledge economy and the importance of lifelong learning. This includes the OECD, United Nations as well as national government bodies, such as the United Kingdom's Department for Education and Employment.

» Our futures rest with ourselves, and to survive the uncertainties we face in our working lives requires us to embrace lifelong learning. Understanding how we learn is an essential component of this, and is discussed in Chapter 6. In addition, the value of the Internet should not be overlooked, as it has a wealth of self-service learning environments. Chapter 4 looks at what the Internet offers.

KEY LEARNING POINTS

» The nature of work has fundamentally changed over the last 250 years – from working with our hands to working with our minds.

» Globalization has resulted in a wealth of competitive forces … it has also allowed corporations to source their products and services where they are cheapest.

» The demographic time bomb ticks louder and louder … where will all the workers come from?

» The very survival of organizations depends on an educated, continuously learning workforce. Skills rapidly become out of date.

» The combined forces of globalization and technological change have increased job insecurity within the white-collar and professional classes.

» Downsizing is likely to be a regular event within most medium to large corporations.

- White-collar work is fast resembling a nineteenth century sweatshop. White-collar work is increasingly stressful, requiring longer hours, less time off and relentless schedules.
- We all should embrace learning, in its widest sense, as a means of safeguarding our corporate futures.

NOTES

1 Cortada, J. (1998) *Rise of the Knowledge Worker*. Butterworth-Heinemann, Woburn MA, pp. 72–9.
2 Jarvis, P. (2001) *Universities and Corporate Universities: The Higher Learning Industry in Global Society*. Kogan Page, London, p. 21.
Hirst, P. & Thompson, P. (1996) *Globalization in Question*. Blackwell, Oxford, p. 18.
3 Source: *The Henley Center*, London, www.henleycentre.com.
4 Wallace, P. (1999) *Agequake: Riding the Demographic Roller Coaster Shaking Business, Finance and Our World*. Nicolas Brealey Publishing, London, p. 3.
5 Andresky Fraser, J. (2001) *White-Collar: The Deterioration of Work and Its Rewards in Corporate America*. W.W. Norton & Co., New York, pp. 3–74.

The E-Dimension

The Internet opens up a wealth of learning opportunities for the lifelong learner. In fact e-learning is big business. However, it is not without issues. This chapter discusses:

» the current issues associated with e-learning;
» how to make e-learning successful;
» what the future may hold; and
» best practice: the US Army.

"The delivery of learning or training using electronically-based approaches – mainly through the Internet, intranet, extranet, or Web."

Martyn Sloman, management writer.

The Internet provides a huge resource for those who pursue lifelong learning. It means individuals are no longer restricted to libraries and books; it means they can share knowledge and learn from others more rapidly than ever before. With millions of sites dedicated to single subjects, chat rooms where it is possible to swap ideas and offer advice, and online universities and other learning resources providing distance learning via the Web, learning has never been easier for the individual. Moreover, the Internet provides a rich environment that can bring the learning process alive with a mix of graphics, self-assessments, video, audio, and real-time interaction.

Naturally, this is not just a resource for the individual. Driven by the need to keep pace with the speed of organizational and technological change, the need to address skills shortages and the need to maintain a knowledgeable and capable workforce, corporations are turning to e-learning in large numbers. And, there are plenty of suppliers, universities and even corporate universities offering a wealth of learning opportunities for those who seek them (see Chapter 9 for some useful learning Websites).

E-learning is big business. The International Data Corporation predicts that there will be a 95 per cent increase in the volume of Internet based training between 1997 and 2002.[1] The IDC also predicts that the European market will be worth $4 billion by 2004.[2] The United States corporate e-learning market was $1.1 billion in 2000 and it is expected to grow to $11.4 billion by 2003. The global market for e-learning is expected to grow to $365 billion by 2003.[3]

No longer constrained by the training room and offsite events, electronic forms of learning can offer distinct advantages to both the organization and the individual, including:

» a 40–60 per cent reduction in costs when compared to classroom learning.[4] This is expected to lead to a drop in classroom-based learning from approximately 78 per cent in 2000 to 4 per cent in 2001,[5] although this does seem to be an incredible drop;

» training courses that can be pushed to all corners of the corporation via the desktop;
» personalized learning that allows employees to tailor their learning needs to meet their specific requirements, learning style and pace;
» any location training and learning (see the best practice box on the United States Army's response to e-learning);
» just-in-time delivery, which is especially important within all major change and technology projects;
» bringing companies and universities together to provide effective business related learning content in a virtual sense;[6] and
» changing the role of the tutor from information provider to mentor.

LEARNING ON DEMAND

The National Technological University[7]

The National Technological University (NTU) in the United States is a prime example of what can be achieved by electronic forms of learning. Born out of a joint venture between nine academic institutions and industry, the NTU was launched in 1984 with over $1 million in start-up capital and became the first accredited virtual university. The concept was very simple in that engineers would have access to the best professors and academics available. Initially this contact was through video tapes of lectures, but over the years the NTU has applied the latest technologies to the concept, moving from videos to satellite uploads of live lectures where remote observers are able to pose questions to the lecturer, and using compressed video images which can be viewed over the Web. In July 1999, NTU acquired the assets of PBS The Business Channel, a leading provider of training for the corporate market. More recently, the NTU changed its name to Stratys to reflect its broader scope, which now encapsulate e-learning and distance learning.

Stratys (NTU) has been incredibly successful, with 52 universities offering over 1300 academic courses, 19 master's degree programs, over 500 professional development courses, and in excess of 200 Web-delivered courses and programs to over 200 major corporations and government bodies and 100,000 technical professionals. This type of learning is also well received by those that use it. As well as providing just-in-time training and education, the majority of students are able to immediately use their new-found knowledge in the workplace.

Visit the Stratys Website at www.ntu.com.

CURRENT ISSUES

With e-learning still in its infancy, it is not without its problems. The very fact that the electronic channel can be used for learning does not mean that learning will take place, or that the e-learning environment will be as good as it should be. According to Dr Roger Shank of Yale University, the conventional business view is that e-learning is just about replicating the classroom on the desktop. This fails to live up to the power of what the e-channel can provide. Shank believes that the current poor level of quality on most online courses has put the learning industry back ten years. Other issues are as follows.

» E-learning can be an isolated experience for the learner and may result in them failing to complete the course. This is reflected in the high dropout rates amongst those using online learning.
» E-learning is impacting upon the training profession, in that it is having to reinvent itself and become an online training provider. This raises questions over the role of the trainer/tutor. No longer an information provider, they must become online tutors and coaches. For some this will prove to be a difficult and painful transition.
» E-learning has to overcome a number of misconceptions including:
  » the belief that e-learning cannot be real learning because it does not involve the physical presence of a tutor;
  » the belief that e-learning provides an opportunity for people to shirk their training responsibilities; and
  » the belief that it is really only designed for the young.

» Those undertaking e-learning who feel that their company is offering an opportunity because it is cheaper than the classroom alternative tend to give it a wide berth.

» Creating an effective e-learning solution is one thing, but keeping it up to date is clearly another. On one hand the e-space provides an excellent opportunity for the organization to provide just-in-time and on-demand training that is able to keep up with changing corporate and strategic aims. On the other, it is clear that organizations find the process of collecting, maintaining and retiring their electronic data a significant overhead. Consider the following statistics:

  » In 1990 the typical Fortune 500 company stored 33 billion characters of electronic data, and in 2010 this is expected to be 400 trillion[8];

  » The volume of corporate information is doubling every 12 months. In addition, the rate at which it is growing is accelerating[9];

  » 77 per cent of organizations publish out-of-date information on their Website[10];

  » 41 per cent of organizations believe that information is duplicated across their sites; and

  » 83 per cent of organizations claim their Website is an important business tool.

» With so much data and information swilling around the corporation there is a real danger of information overload translating into training and learning overload. And in any case, the value of an e-learning solution ultimately resides in the currency, usefulness and appropriateness of its content. If any of these fall short, it is likely that the e-learning solution itself will fall short.

» Organizations face a tough time when developing their own tailored e-learning solutions. This is because they are designed to capture that knowledge which is unique to them – it is their competitive advantage. In such instances it may be possible to outsource general learning, such as management training, financial skills and so on. But proprietary knowledge is better sourced and developed internally or through a partnership arrangement with a professional e-learning provider.

Despite the obstacles, it is possible to work wonders with e-learning, as the following best practice vignette demonstrates.

Every soldier that enrolls onto the program is provided with a technology package that includes a laptop, printer, Internet service provider account, e-mail account and live technology support. In addition, four levels of tutor support are available.

» AUAO level – which provides basic enrollment support to ensure personnel understand the commitment required to complete their course of study and matching courses to individual learning needs.
» Degree level – once enrolled on a degree or certificate program, mentors monitor and track an individual's progress through the degree or certificate, and manage issues associated with the institutions involved.
» Course level – online tutors are available to all students.
» Subject level – course level support is augmented by twenty-four hours a day tutoring services from Smarthinking.com for core courses such as economics and mathematics as well as an online writing lab and research tools.

The army anticipates that within the first three months after launch, 15,000 to 20,000 soldiers will enroll. The long-term vision is to have all of the army's one million personnel taking advantage of the opportunity.

The United States Army's Website can be visited at www.earmyu.com

It is clear that e-learning offers a wealth of learning opportunities for the lifelong learner, whether they are studying on their own, or part of a corporation's attempt to instill lifelong learning within their workforce. It is also clear that e-learning is very different from the standard forms of training and education we have been used to, and because of this it can present problems in implementation.

There are of course plenty of learning solutions and service providers, ranging from consultancies to organizations that will develop and host e-learning environments. A number of these have been listed in Chapter 9, the resources chapter.

And, finally, before we get too excited about e-learning here are some figures about where it currently stands against traditional face-to-face means of learning.[11]

» Just under 84 per cent of training managers still use face-to-face courses in preference to e-learning.
» A little over 45 per cent said they had never used the Internet for e-learning.
» Only 16 per cent use the Internet regularly.

MAKING E-LEARNING SUCCESSFUL

Making e-learning work is a significant undertaking, and one that can involve considerable investment, especially when the technological costs and development time are considered. And it should be emphasized that e-learning is different from traditional forms of learning. The following paragraphs outline some of the current thinking on how to make e-learning a success.

Readiness assessments

To help organizations establish effective e-learning solutions, Samantha Chapnick of Research Dog LLC (www.researchdog.com) has developed an e-learning readiness model that scores an organization's readiness along eight dimensions:

» psychological readiness, which includes assessing the learning population's needs in terms of learning styles, sociability (learning solo or in groups) and acceptance of technology based training;
» sociological readiness, which assesses how people react to the learning environment in its widest sense;
» environmental readiness, which looks at the size, geographical location and educational ability of the learning population, as well as the political barriers to success;
» human resource readiness, that considers the wider support mechanisms of e-learning such as provision of helpdesks, evidence of an e-learning champion/director and so on;
» financial readiness, which addresses the financial implications and investment needs of e-learning;

» technological skill readiness, which assesses the general level of IT literacy within the learning population;

» equipment readiness, which covers the technological requirements of e-learning; and

» content readiness, which assesses the learning material itself, how it is presented, how often it has to be updated, whether it has to be tailored to an individual learner's needs and so on.

Anyone considering developing and implementing an e-learning solution would be wise to use Chapnick's assessment tool before embarking on their investment.

Getting it together

Martyn Sloman, author of *The E-learning Revolution*, believes an effective e-learning system must incorporate six components.[12]

» Context – any e-learning system needs to be tailored to the organization or individual's context otherwise it loses its value and relevance.

» Content – content is of course critical to any learning event, irrespective to how it is delivered. In the case of the electronic channel, content can be provided internally (organizationally specific information and other material) as well as externally (more general material provided by universities, business schools and specialized content providers).

» Community – knowing who will use the system, whether it will be on a single site, multiple sites and so on is an essential element to know how to meet learning demand.

» Behavior and usage analysis – essentially a feedback mechanism for assessing the effectiveness of the system, including what is accessed, for how long, who has accessed it and so on. This will ultimately feed back into the system's structure and content and is critical to keeping it current and useful to the corporation and individual.

» Personalization – if the system is to be capable of delivering real learning, it has to be personalized to individual learning needs, style and pace.

» Infrastructure – linking the e-learning system and the training/learning it provides to other organizational systems and processes is an important way in which to maintain its relevance. In particular, it should be linked to strategy, performance measurement and the annual appraisal process.

Developing e-courses

The best e-courses are those that follow Shank's FREEDOM model and allow for:

» Failure. It is failure that brings out true learning.
» Reasoning. The material should allow the student to apply principles to the course material.
» Emotional impact. Emotion is an essential component of the learning process.
» Exploration. Allowing the student to learn through discovery, rather than prescription.
» Doing. Being active is fundamental to reinforcing concepts and learning.
» Observation. This helps to decode what is going on in the real world.
» Motivation. You need to understand why you are learning something to be able to learn it.

Keeping it current

And finally, it is essential to keep the information and knowledge used within the e-learning environment up to date. From time to time, it is a good idea to ask the following questions that are based on those recommended by Alastair Rylatt, author of *Learning Unlimited*[1]

» Is the current knowledge within the organization good enough?
» Where do we need more content and how do we source it – internally or externally?
» Where do we need to target our training and learning so that we can develop our people more quickly?
» Are staffers receiving the learning they need?
» Are we keeping our learning materials up to date? (See Chapter 8 and the entry on the information life cycle).

LOOKING TO THE FUTURE

According to a recent report to the US Congress,[13] over the next three to five years advances in technology will provide more attractive and sophisticated solutions to support lifelong learning. This will be possible through increased bandwidth, the expansion of broadband and wireless computing, digital convergence and lowering connectivity costs. More important perhaps will be the emergence of technical standards capable of creating a consistent environment for learning over the Web. This will eliminate the current variable nature of the content of most learning sites. Some is clearly very good; much is mediocre. Content management systems will increasingly complement learning management systems. The latter concentrate on the administrative aspects of learning, such as enrollment, student and instructor logistics, but are not designed to address issues of scalability, reuse and personalization. Effective e-learning requires content management systems that create, manage, deliver and maintain Web-based content for learning. Combining learning and content management systems will provide a more powerful learning environment than we have today.

KEY LEARNING POINTS
The e-dimension

» E-learning solutions offer much wider and richer possibilities for the lifelong learner.
» E-learning provides anytime, anywhere, just-in-time training and education.
» Leading edge organizations are embracing e-learning as a way of maintaining a well educated and flexible workforce.
» E-learning is very different from traditional forms of education and as such there are risks to overcome when implementing it. The use of Research Dog's e-learning assessment can be an effective means of understanding these risks.
» To be successful, e-learning depends on excellent content that is up to date and leading edge.
» The significance of e-learning will increase as systems become more sophisticated and effective.
» In the short-term e-learning will not replace traditional forms of learning.

NOTES

1. Rylatt, A. (2001) *Learning Unlimited: Transforming Learning in the Workplace*, 2nd edn. Kogan Page, London, p. 151.

2. Lowe, J. (2001) "Message management." *People Performance,* April, pp. 53–54.

3. The power of the Internet for learning: moving from promise to practice. Report of the Web-based Education Committee to the President and the Congress of the United States, December (2000), p. 8.

4. Towner, N. (2001) "Remote control." *e.businessreview*, June (2001), p. 36.

5. The power of the Internet for learning: moving from promise to practice. Report of the Web-based Education Committee to the President and the Congress of the United States, December (2000), p. 8.

6. Little, B. (2001) "Do gooder." *People Performance,* April, pp. 44–45.

7. Tapscott, D. (1996) *The Digital Economy: Promise and Peril in the Age of Networked Intelligence*. McGraw Hill, New York, pp. 210–212.

8. Wind, J.Y. & Main, J. (1998) *Driving Change: How the Best Companies are Preparing for the 21st Century*. Kogan Page, London, pp. 158.

9. Newing, R. (1999) "Taking the paranoia out of knowledge acquisition." *Financial Times*, April 28.

10. This point and the following two bullet points in the list come from: Vowler, J. (2000) "Testing time for e-commerce." *Computer Weekly*, October **19**, p. 70.

11. From "E-Briefs." *People Performance*, June (2001), p. 8.

12. Sloman, M. (2001) *The E-learning Revolution: From Propositions to Action*. Institute of Personnel and Development, London, pp. 44–47.

13. The power of the Internet for learning: moving from promise to practice. Report of the Web-based Education Committee to the President and the Congress of the United States, December (2000).

The Global Dimension

Globalization has been the principal driver behind lifelong learning because it has exposed nations, organizations and individuals to levels of competition and change they have not been used to. This chapter outlines:

» how nations are responding;
» how corporations are exploiting learning opportunities globally;
» the emergence of the global talent pool and what it means for those with the appropriate skills;
» best practice: ABB; and
» the cultural dimension to learning.

"Globalization is the latest stage in a long accumulation of technological advance which has given human beings the ability to
conduct their affairs across the world without reference to nationality, government authority, time of day or physical environment."
Richard Langhorne, management writer.

". . . when it comes to globalization, a company's people are more
important than its products."
*John Micklethwait & Adrian Wooldridge, journalists and
authors.*

The global dimension to lifelong learning may at first appear to be
insignificant, but it is in fact one of the major driving forces behind
nations and organizations becoming more interested in the capabilities
of their staff, especially their ability to learn and change.

THE NATIONS AWAKE

The need to have an ever-increasing pool of knowledgeable, flexible
and productive workers is not lost on the policy makers. They realize
that the ultimate survival of their nation depends on their ability to
compete. And to compete in the future they need to be developing the
next generation of capable and adaptable employees, entrepreneurs
and business leaders. Furthermore, they need to ensure that they can
attract talented people to their shores. This is especially important
for the industrialized countries because their populations are ageing
so rapidly (see Chapter 3). Therefore, taxation (both corporate and
personal), inward investment and immigration policies need to be
sufficiently flexible to bring new talent in and stop existing talent from
seeping out.

According to the International Congress on Technical and Vocational
Education held in South Korea in April 1999, central to the effort to
compete in the twenty-first century is the preparation of a productive,
flexible workforce. And every country will be obliged to enable its
citizens to acquire the skills necessary to survive and to improve their
quality of life because the demands of the workplace are likely to leave
people without skills unemployed and unemployable.

Policy makers believe that lifelong learning is a long-term task that
has to be achieved in two stages. The first, and possibly the most

essential, is to ensure that people leave their formal education as lifelong learners. This must equip everyone with the motivation and basic skills with which to direct their own learning for the rest of their working lives.

The second stage is to ensure that adults have access to the learning they need. Although governments are beginning to provide such access through the provision of tax credits that can be used to offset the costs of learning, these are often quite limited in their scope. For example, from July 1, 1998 United States' taxpayers were eligible to claim a non-refundable Lifetime Learning Credit against their federal income taxes. Up to the end of 2002, the Lifetime Learning Credit is equivalent to 20 per cent of the taxpayer's first $5,000 out-of-pocket expenses, and after 2002 this rises to 20 per cent of the first $10,000. Therefore, the maximum credit a taxpayer can claim is $1,000 until 2002 and $2,000 thereafter. The United Kingdom's equivalent of this is the Individual Learning Account, a one-off payment of £150 towards tuition.

GLOBAL LEARNING IN CORPORATIONS

According to Dr David Hennessey, associate professor of marketing and international business at Babson College in the United States, globalization has enhanced the corporation's and individual's opportunity to learn and share knowledge. For example, Hewlett-Packard was able to re-engineer its Canadian-designed small printers to include fewer parts and reduce assembly times. Thorn's Nordic subsidiary found that its rental customers were not concerned about having emergency repairs on the day their appliance failed. Global testing found that this was true across the world. As a result the company reduced the number of engineers on 24-hour callout and redirected this saving into offering those customers in financial difficulties a one-month payment holiday.[1]

Of course, organizations are not responding out of choice; globalization has forced them to confront inefficiencies that come to light at all levels. Not only are the general problems of uncompetitive process, outdated management and organizational structures exposed, but so are the lack of new skills, attitudes and behaviors that make organizations globally competitive. Those organizations that fail to find and develop their workforce will ultimately be overtaken by those that can.

This heightened competitiveness has meant that organizations have had to turn to more effective means of maintaining and developing their human capital so that they can respond more rapidly to changes, the majority of which have been brought about by technological change. In particular they are turning to their own brand of university, the corporate university, which is discussed in Chapter 6.

WELCOME TO THE GLOBAL TALENT POOL

In the past, developing nations were an abundant source of natural resources. Today they are an abundant source of skilled and cheap labor. This last point is especially relevant to those in the industrialized world with outdated skills, as organizations will not think twice about moving their production facilities elsewhere as the following examples show.[2]

» In 1960, 100 per cent of Motorola's workforce resided in the United States. Today, the figure is only 44 per cent. The rest are scattered around the world, and it is now one of the largest employers in Malaysia.
» General Electric is the largest employer in Singapore.
» In 1990, AT&T closed its transformer factory in Radford, Virginia eliminating 2,100 jobs. These were moved to factories in Mexico, where workers were paid $2.35 per hour compared to the $13 per hour paid to its Virginian workforce.

The source of cheap labor has changed locations around the world. Starting in Hong Kong, then moving to Taiwan and Thailand, it has now shifted to China and India, where labor is cheaper still. This is the way of the world for the commoditized, low-skilled labor associated with manufacturing.

Such moves are a great way to drive out costs and increase margins. And as the abilities of the developing nations increase, they will begin to take on knowledge work, the very stuff of our survival. Richard Langhorne, author of *The Coming of Globalization*, believes that the technological advances in communications (leading to globalization) have significantly increased the economic asset represented by knowledge and downgraded the importance of things. It also means that knowledge is no longer constrained by its location – it is universally accessible. The combination of globalization and technological advance has allowed highly qualified people within developing countries, such as India, to compete on the global jobs market. For example, the Indian IT market is growing significantly, and undertakes software development projects at a fraction of the usual cost. And, of course, for those people in the industrialized world with hot skills they too can work literally anywhere. This is particularly true of consultants, investment bankers, and IT professionals. As individuals, it is important to understand what skills and attributes we have and what is in demand, as this is the only way to assess our position within the global talent pool, and depending on where you sit, determines how you can exploit it. It also highlights what else you might need to learn to be able to join.

ABB, GLOBAL LEARNING AND THE GLOBAL CITIZEN

ABB, the Swedish corporation, typifies the type of consistency any organization that trades globally aspires to. Since its creation through the merger of ASEA of Sweden and Brown Boveri & Company of Switzerland, it has achieved an amazing degree of convergence and consistency across a wide range of countries and cultures. Although it has acquired and merged with many companies from around the world, it has preserved and promoted the national cultures of each. But as well as preserving the local cultures, ABB has developed a global culture that ensures it does not fracture into national islands. So, although factories are spread around the world, they all form part of global groups that share technology and best practice.

Cross border co-operation is also enhanced through the use of multicultural teams. Few of ABB's 5000 profit centers are viable as stand alone entities – they depend on each other for ideas, information and resources. This engenders a spirit of learning, connectivity and collaboration, vital to the success of the global firm.

ABB recognizes that global leaders have to be developed, and of their 25,000 leaders, approximately 500 are destined at any one time to be global leaders. This group are nurtured at an early stage and transferred to other countries to gain the necessary cultural experience and learning to make them successful. Of course ABB's success is not just down to leadership. The workers themselves also benefit through continuous training, which has been increased by a factor of four in recent years. This learning is predominantly action learning (see Chapter 8) and is often global, with staff from one country being educated in another.

The following quote sums up the importance of cultural sensitivity to ABB:[3]

> "Because you must listen to different cultures – to see why a Pole or a Russian or a Chinese thinks the way they do. You have to understand different cultures if you work in a global company... Global strategy is the distillation of thousands and thousands of local decisions made each day."

Ultimately, ABB's success is down to cross-country learning and a strong culture of collaboration and global/local citizenship.[4]

THE CULTURAL DIMENSION TO LEARNING

As we have seen for those of us with skills and knowledge that are in demand, it is possible to work without frontiers. And for those working in multinational and transnational corporations, tours of duty overseas are often part of the process of becoming a global citizen and a necessary step for moving up the hierarchy.

However, Terrence Deal and Allan Kennedy, authors of *The New Corporate Cultures* believe that the global economy has caused severe strains on corporate cultures. They believe that rapid globalization has caught people unprepared for confusing cross-cultural business transactions and has resulted in the tendency to stereotype. Therefore, to succeed in a global workplace, we must embrace another aspect to our lifelong learning: understanding national cultures.

Thankfully, some of the most enlightening and useful research on national culture is available to us all. Hofstede, who studied 116,000

IBM employees around the world who were identical in terms of position, and role and only differed in respect of their nationality, has identified four dimensions of national culture.[5]

» The power distance. Hofstede defined this as the extent to which the less powerful members of institutions and organizations within a country expect and accept that power is distributed unequally. In practice this means the degree to which subordinates are willing to question their superiors and push back against decisions. Such push back is more prevalent in western societies and less common in the Far East. Furthermore, where the acceptance of inequality is greatest, paternalistic and autocratic management styles tend to dominate, whilst the opposite is true in those countries where inequality is less acceptable. In such countries management tends to be more consultative. This is typical of the Low Countries, such as the Netherlands.

» Individualism – collectivism. This refers to the extent to which people within a society are expected to fend for themselves and their immediate families. The more one is expected to fend for oneself, the more individualistic the society. The opposite of this is collectivism, where from birth, people are integrated into strong, cohesive groups which tend to be maintained throughout life. As to be expected, in those societies that are more collective, decision making tends to be group based, and as a consequence often slower (for example, the Nordic countries) than in those countries that are more individualistic (for example, the United States and the United Kingdom).

» Masculinity–femininity. In those societies that can be considered masculine, emphasis tends to be placed on achievement, ambition and success (for example, the United States), whilst in those countries that are more feminine, the emphasis is on quality of work and caring for others (for example, Finland, Holland, and Sweden). As expected, in those countries that are more masculine, working hours tend to be longer (witness, for example the United Kingdom, which has the longest working hours in Europe; 91 per cent of British managers now work more than their contracted hours), whilst in more feminine countries work is a means to an end, not the end itself.

» Uncertainty avoidance. This refers to the extent to which members of a culture feel threatened by uncertain or unknown circumstances. In those countries where uncertainty avoidance is high, people attempt to reduce it through structure, process and familiarity so that events are clearly interpretable. This is true of Germany, Switzerland and France. In addition, where uncertainty avoidance is high, people are less likely to question superiors and tend to avoid situations that involve conflict. In those countries that have a weak uncertainty avoidance, there tends to be less concern or need for strict rules; people are generally more self-governing, conflict is seen as non-threatening and an important part of the workplace. Furthermore, individuals are generally more flexible. This is typical of the United States, United Kingdom and Australia.

Taking the data and insights that Hofstede so meticulously put together provides the would-be globe-trotting employee with the basics for managing the cultural differences they are likely to encounter. For those who work on global engagements, such as consultants, Hofstede's work is a great starting point for managing multicultural teams.

KEY LEARNING POINTS

» The globalization of commerce has created an uncertain future for us all.
» For those with skills that are transferable and in demand, globalization offers the opportunity to work without frontiers.
» Being successful in the global workplace means becoming culturally intelligent.

NOTES

1 See www.ashridge.com/directions.
2 Deal, T. & Kennedy, A. (1999) *The New Corporate Cultures*. Orion Business Books, London, p. 155.
3 Barham, K. & Heimer, C. (1998) *ABB, the Dancing Giant: Creating the Globally Connected Corporation*. Financial Times/Prentice Hall, London, p. 345.

4 Sources: Barham, K. & Heimer, C. (1998) *ABB, the Dancing Giant: Creating the Globally Connected Corporation*, Financial Times/Prentice Hall, London; and Dauphinais, W. & Price, C. (1998) *Straight from the CEO*. Nicholas Brealey, London, pp. 37–46.

5 Hofstede, G. (1994) *Cultures and Organization: Intercultural Cooperation and Its Importance for Survival*. Harper Collins Business, London.

The State of the Art

To succeed at lifelong learning we need to consider how we learn and overcome our barriers to learning. For the organization, this also means creating an environment in which their employees can learn. This chapter discusses:

» the major barriers to learning;
» four models of learning; and
» the rise and importance of corporate universities.

"In your career, knowledge is like milk. It has a shelf life stamped right on the carton. The shelf life of a degree in engineering is about three years. If you're not replacing everything you know by then, your career is gong to turn sour fast."

Louis Ross, Chief Technical Officer, Ford Motor Company.[1]

It is increasingly recognized that although organizations can gain competitive advantage through being first to market with new technologies, this advantage is often short lived, and easy to replicate. Furthermore, the rate of technological change often means today's technology is obsolete tomorrow. Organizations are instead turning to their intangible assets (i.e. their staff) as a means of establishing and maintaining their competitive advantage. In the same vein, we as individuals can set ourselves aside from the competition by developing our skills and knowledge so that we too create and maintain our personal competitive advantage. As Tom Peters puts it – creating BrandU. But the only way to achieve this is to embrace lifelong learning in its widest sense.

The following paragraphs cover three major themes within lifelong learning: overcoming our learning obstacles; understanding how we learn; and, the increasing importance of corporate universities.

STARTING OUT – OVERCOMING OUR LEARNING OBSTACLES

Peter Senge in his book, *The Fifth Discipline*, described a number of learning obstacles that reduce our ability to learn and which ultimately prevent the creation of the learning organization.

» I am my position. This refers to the way we become defined by our job and how it can be very difficult to do anything else or think outside the confines of our immediate role. This tends to be reinforced by the culture of the individual functions people work within and the technical training they receive. In extreme cases this can be perpetuated as people move up the organization. For example, if we consider most career routes, they tend to remain within a single discipline, such as finance or information technology. This can act as a major barrier to learning and lead to blind spots in knowledge. In particular, such blind spots tend to arise at times of crisis where stress and anxiety prevent learning (this is an automatic, physiological response of the brain, which shuts down the reasoning capability in favor of a fight or flight response).

» The enemy is out there. This is a by-product of "I am my position" and is associated with blaming others when things go wrong. This is very common in organizations where one function blames another or when a project, product or process fails. We become so embroiled in our narrowly focused roles that we fail to see the wider issues involved. As a result we fail to learn from the experience or see the other function's perspective. This ensures that we end up repeating the same mistakes time and time again. In addition, too many organizations have a blame culture that prevents learning when things don't go according to plan. As a result people fail to take risks because of the implications of failure. And, when things do go wrong every effort is made to find a suitable scapegoat rather than directing energy towards the learning required to ensure the same mistake is not repeated. See Chapter 8 and the after action review technique as one way to overcome this type of learning disability.

» The delusion of learning from experience. Increasingly, and especially within work, there is no direct link between the actions we take and the outcomes that occur. And although we learn best from direct experience this is rarely the case within the organizational setting. To address this we must seek feedback from those around us so that we are able to learn from experience. Being a small cog in a large wheel usually limits an individual's ability to see the bigger picture.

» We fail to see the long-cycle changes. With the pace of work speeding up and our obsession with getting things done at an ever-faster rate, we often fail to see the long-term changes. Indeed we often dismiss them as irrelevant. This is leading organizations and individuals alike to dismiss the benefits of strategy and planning. But without strategies or plans, it can be very difficult to gauge the results of action and learn from the experience. As we will see in Chapter 10, planning is an essential component to lifelong learning.

» Inaction and the knowing–doing gap. We all suffer from knowing that we should do something but failing to do it. We all avoid difficult situations, and we are all guilty of procrastination. The same applies to organizations that skirt round or spend endless amounts of time discussing problems and their underlying components rather than solving them. This type of inactivity fails us all, and even though many people know that lifelong learning is an important building block for their future, very few embrace it . . . they know they should do, but they don't.

Senge believes that those who are keen to learn (and hence willing to overcome their barriers to learning) should embrace the following disciplines.

» They should update their mental models, removing those that are outdated and no longer suited to the modern workplace (see Chapter 8 and the entry on neurolinguistic programming).
» They should be open with other people (share knowledge, take feedback and so on).
» They should understand how their organization really works, including the political and power dimensions (this is Senge's "fifth discipline"; being able to see patterns and systemic relationships); they should develop a shared vision.
» They should then work to achieve the common purpose defined within that vision.

The problem facing all lifelong learners is to accept that the learning process is different from the learning we experienced at school and university. It is a shame that many people have been switched-off from learning by the process they went through during their teens and early twenties. Many tend to it as a formal event that is dry and not particularly enjoyable. Alastair Rylatt, author of *Learning Unlimited*, believes a wounded learner is no different from someone who has been physically hurt, and to improve their health requires effort in order to understand why they have problems with learning and to make them more aware of their motivations and learning preferences. The use of a personal coach (see Chapter 7 and 10) can be an effective way to overcome such problems and get the best out of learning.

UNDERSTANDING HOW WE LEARN

Any discussion about lifelong learning would be incomplete without some mention of the process of learning. This is important because of its centrality to being successful at lifelong learning. If we are unaware of how we learn it can be very difficult for us to take the deliberate steps required to progress. The following paragraphs summarize four models.

» The four stages of learning (and unlearning).
» Learning preferences and neurolinguistic programming.
» The multiple intelligence model of Howard Gardner.
» The Kolb learning cycle.

The four stages of learning

When we learn anything, we typically pass through four distinct phases.

» Unconscious incompetence – we don't know that we don't know. We have yet to learn about a subject, such as driving a car or riding a bike.
» Conscious incompetence – as we begin to learn something, we are acutely aware of our failings and inability to master the skill we are trying to learn.
» Conscious competence – we have begun to master the skill but still have to maintain our concentration and are still prone to errors. It is believed that it is during this stage we learn the most.
» Unconscious competence – this is where we apply the skill automatically without the need to really think about it. The unconscious mind takes control leaving the conscious mind to think about other things.

The inherent danger of always operating at the unconsciously competent level is that we can develop bad habits and fail to change as the environment around us changes. Therefore, it is sometimes necessary to unlearn what we already know and relearn it taking into account the changes around us. And, because it can be very difficult for us to see the need to change, it can be beneficial to seek feedback from peers, or a personal coach to help identify where change (and hence relearning) is required. In this case it is necessary to step back through the stages until you reach conscious incompetence and then rebuild up to the final level, conscious competence.

Learning styles and neurolinguistic programming

Neurolinguistic programming has identified three preferences for the way we learn: visual, auditory and kinaesthetic. Visual learners prefer the use of pictures, models and graphs. They prefer to see the whole picture, rather than parts of it, so context tends to be very important when learning. Auditory learners prefer to learn in a lecture setting, as they learn more from what is said than what is shown. They value explanation and discussion rather than images or textbooks. Finally, kinaesthetic learners prefer more tactile forms of learning and learning by doing. The kinaesthetic learner prefers activities and exercises that illustrate a point or help to reinforce what has already been said. Ideally any programs of learning should cater for all three modes of learning, and we should all understand our own preferences.

Multiple intelligences

The notion that the best way to measure someone's ability is through their intelligence quotient (IQ) is gradually eroding. And this has implications for the way that we approach lifelong learning. As the body of research suggesting that the most intelligent people are not necessarily the most successful grows, organizations are recognizing that all-round ability holds the key to their success. And, if that's the case, we should develop all-round skills to maintain our position in the workplace. Howard Gardener of Harvard University offers a richer model that suggests that we all have a mix of nine intelligences.

» Linguistic – this is the ability to understand information in verbal and written form and includes the ability to tell stories, write reports and critically analyze written material. It also encapsulates humor, wit, persuasion and the ability to apply linguistic reasoning to problem solving.
» Mathematical technical – this is the ability to understand descriptions and instructions and includes the ability to solve technical problems using the principles of scientific enquiry, logical thinking, and the ability to make objective decisions. It also encapsulates general financial skills and the basics of project management.

» Visual – as it suggests, this includes all things visual such as the creation of visual representations (graphs, presentations and so on), a concern for aesthetics, and the ability to translate visual representations to the real world and vice versa.

» Auditory – this is associated with having a sensitivity for the dynamics of sound, and is typically found in musicians.

» Kinaesthetic motor – essentially a self-focused sensitivity for the physiological feedback from the body. It also includes the ability to use complex machinery and undertake intricate work.

» Interpersonal – the ability to accurately define the emotions and needs of others. This includes the ability to take into account another persons emotions and having the skill to adjust behavior accordingly. This intelligence, along with intra-personal intelligence, forms the backbone of emotional intelligence (see Chapters 8 and 9) and is one of the essential characteristics of a leader.

» Intra-personal – the ability to know oneself in terms of goals, ambitions, feelings and emotions – also known as the inner game. This encapsulates coping skills, resilience, determination, and represents one of the most significant checks to pure intelligence. Indeed, most very bright people lack this type of intelligence. The key skill of intra-personally intelligent people is the ability to reinvent themselves over time. Given the need to be adaptable and open to change, this is an essential skill for the lifelong learner. Neurolinguistic programming provides the tools and techniques through which this can be achieved (see Chapters 8 and 9).

» Naturalistic – this is associated with the ability to relate to or profit from the natural environment, including its exploitation.

» Philosophical ethical – this refers to the ability to match one's skills and abilities to different environments, particularly cultures. This would include, for example, being sensitive to different national cultures when working on an international assignment (see Chapter 5 for more on cultural intelligence – an important skill within a globalized world). It also extends to having sensitivity for the moral and ethical issues of a situation.

The Kolb learning model

David Kolb's model is probably the most widely known tool for describing the learning process and determining an individual's learning preferences. In a similar vein to the three preferences outlined by neurolinguistic programming, assessing an individual's learning style provides the basis for formulating learning experiences that allow the person to get the most out of the process. According to Kolb, the process of learning follows four steps that form a continuous, never ending process.

» Concrete experience – as this suggests, learning from experience.
» Reflective observation – reflecting on events, considering alternative courses of action and seeking out the meaning of things.
» Abstract conceptualization - formulation of abstract concepts and generalizations through logical analysis.
» Active experimentation – testing the implications of new concepts through deliberate action.

This model suggests that there are four modes of learning that correspond to each of the four stages.

» Activists (corresponds to concrete experience) – these are people who prefer to act rather than think in the learning process. Such people prefer to rely on intuition rather than logic and prefer to learn in a real world setting rather than the classroom. Trial and error is the primary method of learning.
» Reflectors (corresponds to reflection and observation) – these are people who prefer to consider the pros and cons of things, like to take a lot of points of view and information on board before taking action. Such people prefer to learn through observation and from other people. Time is the biggest issue for the reflector, as they need plenty of it within the learning process.
» Theorists (corresponds to abstract conceptualization) – these people learn through abstract thinking and modeling rather than taking action. Theorists prefer to conduct research as part of the learning process.
» Pragmatists (corresponds to active experimentation) – these people learn best by tackling a practical problem. They prefer to be given hints, tips and practical steps to success rather than researching it for themselves. They generally accept received wisdom at face value. Chapter 10 will be particularly relevant to the pragmatists amongst us.

The body of research into learning and learning styles is extremely useful for the lifelong learner for the following reasons.

1 It provides a frame of reference for matching learning to our preferred learning styles.
2 It allows us to develop a rounded approach to our learning by focusing on more than just IQ – we are capable of developing ourselves across many dimensions, as Howard Gardner has demonstrated.
3 It gives us a process for learning.

EMPLOYERS TAKING LEARNING INTO THEIR OWN HANDS – THE RISE OF THE CORPORATE UNIVERSITY

As the industrialized countries have transformed themselves into knowledge-based societies, the demand for new recruits with a higher level of education has increased dramatically. For example, 85 per cent of current jobs in the United States require an education beyond high school level, up from 65 per cent in 1991.[2] The traditional source of educated people, the universities, have themselves changed to accommodate this demand by both catering for a much larger number of entry level students, and offering more in the way of postgraduate courses, including masters and doctorates.[3] In addition, universities are now providing a much higher proportion of practical courses geared toward the needs of the workplace, rather than the generation of an intellectual elite.

But when it comes to lifelong learning the key question yet to be resolved is who should pay the considerable costs involved. Should the public purse pay? All the trends seem to point to no, at least in the United Kingdom and United States, where those taking higher degrees in order to improve employment prospects generally have to fend for themselves. And certainly those who work for themselves have to fund their own development, which, at between $1500 and $3000 per course, is an expensive business.

The introduction of the individual learning account (ILA) in the United Kingdom and its equivalent tax break in the United States provides a minimal level of funding which is just not enough to accomplish real lifelong learning. As for individuals, the costs for the majority are too high and help to limit the level of continuous learning that takes place. With the advent and flexibility of the Internet (see Chapter 6, and Chapter 9) this is changing. But, the bulk of the costs are borne by the employer ... as long as they see a return on their investment. Increasingly, the corporation is taking the matter into their own hands by turning to the concept of the corporate university.

One of the first corporate universities was McDonald's Hamburger University, which opened its doors in the early 1960s. Since then the number of corporate universities has grown steadily as the need for lifelong learning has been recognized as a priority for most corporations. Growing from approximately 400 in 1985, to 1000 in 1995, it is believed that there are now some 2000 corporate universities in existence with an average yearly spend of $10.7 million.[4] It is now estimated that 40 per cent of Fortune 500 companies have established corporate universities, and at the current rate of growth, corporate universities will out number traditional universities by 2010.[5]

According to Chase,[6] the corporate university has seven functions.

» Teaching corporate culture.
» Fostering cross-functional skills.
» Providing a central technology-based training facility.
» Cutting training cycle times.
» Operating training as a fee earning business.
» Providing education for non-employees.
» Developing partnerships with universities and business schools.

Corporate universities are principally designed to provide timely training and education that has been tailored to the specifics of the organization. As a result, they tend to be practical, business focused offerings that reinforce existing competencies and develop new ones. Typical subjects covered by such universities include corporate history; globalization; team working; quality; project and program management; leadership and leadership development as well as a host of functional subjects such as software development; sales and marketing; finance and so on. The basic ethos of the corporate university is that all their workers should be learners all of the time and through this become effective organizational citizens capable of furthering the corporate mission.

Many organizations are building on their experience of operating corporate universities (see summary box) and a small number are implementing more innovative approaches to foster learning. For example, BP Amoco is offering its employees guaranteed time to think and learn by providing them with personal learning days. Others are introducing lifelong learning directors, directors of learning and similar roles. For example, the United Kingdom's Inland Revenue has recently appointed a director of learning.

CORPORATE UNIVERSITIES: RATIONALE, SUCCESS FACTORS AND THE FUTURE

The United Kingdom's Department of Trade and Industry studied a number of corporate universities as part of its report, *The Future of Corporate Learning*. The organizations ranged from utilities such as Anglian Water, banks such as Lloyds TSB, and technology companies such as Motorola. Common themes emerged from the case studies in terms of: the rationale for establishing corporate universities; what the organizations have learnt from the experience (success criteria); and, how they intend to build on their success.

Rationale
1 The need to have a workforce capable of coping with constant change.
2 The importance of knowledge sharing.
3 The need to address skill shortages.
4 Improving access to research and development both locally and globally.
5 Rationalizing the number of course providers and raising quality levels.
6 Enabling greater cross-fertilization of ideas across the business.
7 Creating stronger links between learning and business needs.
8 Keeping pace with technological and organizational change.

Success criteria

1 Learning should be seen to be an integral part of a job not something added to it.
2 It is essential to capture and build upon existing knowledge.
3 Partnerships with academic institutions are mutually beneficial and provide access to the latest research and management thinking.
4 Learning goals should be included within everyone's annual objectives.
5 Senior management support and visibility is key.
6 Courses should be consistent, replicable and capable of being delivered anywhere.

The future

1 Enhancing learning through the web and electronic means.
2 Increasing the number of partnerships with education institutions.
3 Developing measures to assess the return on learning investment.
4 Reducing the cycle time for learning.
5 Encouraging everyone to be responsible for their own learning.

A LOOK TO THE FUTURE

So what of the future of lifelong learning? It is clear that its importance will grow for all stakeholders. The very survival of individuals, corporations and in extreme cases, nations will depend on the ability to continuously learn. With an ageing population, the acceleration of technological change and the competitive forces of globalization, competition for the best talent will hot up. Attracting the best talented people will not only mean rewarding them, it will also mean providing them with learning opportunities throughout their careers. Those nations and corporations that can provide these opportunities will establish a significant competitive advantage over those that don't. As for the individual, it will become increasingly necessary to embrace lifelong learning especially as knowledge work will become the driving force of the global economy. For those of us that choose to learn continuously the rewards will be great. Not only will we be able to maintain an unbroken career, we ought to be able to pick and choose the best jobs – globally.

Over the next five to ten years the significance of the Internet as a practical and valuable source of learning will grow. Smart use of content and learning management systems that can adjust to the learning needs and styles of the learner will mean better take-up. The rise of the corporate university will continue and the traditional universities will transform themselves to compete. Organizations will begin to appoint chief learning officers and directors of learning whose sole responsibility will be to ensure the correct processes and mechanisms are in place to allow individuals and organizations to learn. As we will see in Chapter 7, some organizations and individuals are already responding.

KEY LEARNING POINTS

» Before we can become successful at lifelong learning we need to overcome our learning obstacles.
» Success means understanding our learning preferences and matching our learning experiences to them.
» Lifelong learning requires a significant commitment, especially financial.
» Organizations have taken the lead in lifelong learning through the introduction of corporate universities.
» The future will require individuals and organizations alike to become expert lifelong learners.

NOTES

1 Quoted in Tapscott, D. (1996) *The Digital Economy: Promise and Peril in the Age of Networked Intelligence*. McGraw Hill, New York, pp. 198–199.

2 The power of the Internet for learning: moving from promise to practice. Report of the Web-based Education Committee to the President and the Congress of the United States, December (2000).

3 Jarvis, P. (2001) *Universities and Corporate Universities: The Higher Learning Industry in Global Society*. Kogan Page, London, pp. 1–29.

4 *Ibid.* pp. 104–113.

5 The power of the Internet for learning: moving from promise to practice. Report of the Web-based Education Committee to the President and the Congress of the United States, December (2000), p. 8.

6 Chase, N. (1998) ''Lessons from the corporate university.'' *Quality Magazine*, June.

In Practice: Success Stories

Being successful at lifelong learning can be viewed from two dimensions, the corporate and the individual. And success means many things – having the right learning infrastructure, encouraging employees to learn continuously, and getting the necessary support through coaching. This chapter therefore includes:

» a case study of Barclays Corporate Banking;
» a case study of a major communications company;
» a case study of a global management consultancy;
» a case study of coaching (The Leverage Organization); and
» a case study of self development – Jan Hennessey.

"Organizations learn only through individuals who learn. Individual learning does not guarantee organizational learning. But without it no organizational learning occurs."

Peter Senge, systems thinker and management guru.

As corporations struggle with increasing competition and the need to continually update the skills of their staff, they see learning and plenty of it as the solution. In addition, as individuals recognize that their careers depend on their ability to learn and reinvent themselves, they too are turning to lifelong learning as the means through which they can achieve this. The following vignettes illustrate what is being done to generate a continuous learning culture within organizations, and how individuals are responding.

BARCLAYS CORPORATE BANKING

Barclays is one of the United Kingdom's largest financial services organizations. It has around 70,000 staff and operates globally. Around 50,000 staff work in the UK. In addition, Barclays has major international operations in Africa, the Caribbean, Spain, France, Portugal, USA and Hong Kong.

The challenge

In 1998, Barclays reorganized itself into two operating units, retail banking and corporate banking. No change of this magnitude had ever been introduced into Barclays before. Nevertheless, a combination of competition, globalization of financial services, the Internet revolution and the lessons learnt in the recession of the early 1990s meant that such change was inevitable. Essentially the traditional regionalized structure of Barclays was to be entirely dismantled and a new integrated corporate banking business (along with a new retail structure) established in its place. The shift to the integrated corporate banking business affected 12,000 staff and required them to adjust to new organizational structures, processes and objectives. The objectives of the new business were threefold.

» Establish a new operating model, based upon delivery through cross-functional processes, and migrate existing employees into it whilst delivering unchanged customer service.

» Realize productivity improvements of 10 per cent.
» Establish a high performance culture.

The solution

Supporting the staff through the change was critical and it was heavily focused on training, development and creating a culture of lifelong learning. This was initially achieved by the following.

» Developing a new performance management system around key business, leadership and personal imperatives.
» Reconfiguring training to align it with the business and deliver it centrally.
» Developing an intranet learning center, providing access to tools for assessing career and learning needs. This self-development toolkit included a 360-degree feedback tool, self-assessment audits, links to external Websites, and tools to determine leadership and personal imperatives. All of these were mapped to opportunities, and supported by videos, courses and key actions that could be undertaken by the individual.
» Developing and rolling out a staff survey to assess how Barclays was performing against a basket of measures that included learning and development. The purpose of this was to benchmark Barclays against the rest of UK business and use this to update the change agenda.
» Performing organization and management reviews in order to review talent against the organizational structure and objectives as a feed into the development of personal development plans.
» Introducing a development center for high potential groups to create gold standard personal development plans.

Benefits

Establishing direct causal links between business outcomes and the adoption of a lifelong learning ethos has not been easy, as this was just one component of the wider change program. However, Barclays has achieved much over the past three years.

» Three thriving new businesses have been established from the old regional set-up. Income is at record levels.

» Line responsibility for pay and reward and personal responsibility for career development is a way of life.
» Costs have been maintained and productivity improvements held.
» Customer satisfaction ratings are at an all time high.
» The staff survey has shown more rapid improvement than the consultants used had ever seen before. Against the majority of the categories used Barclays are truly "world class."

The future

Barclays is now following two strategies in relation to lifelong learning. The first involves reconfiguring its learning offerings through the creation of Barclays University, which is currently being piloted. This supports the second and more complex strategy of changing the way people view their careers. The changing economic and competitive environments mean that Barclays, as with all other organizations, can no longer guarantee a job for life. Increasingly, staff are being encouraged to manage their own careers and the learning and self-development that goes with it. In addition, managers will be expected to provide learning support and coaching to their staff as Barclays creates an environment that encourages personal responsibility for career management and learning.

A MAJOR US COMMUNICATIONS ORGANIZATION

This fast growing Internet communications company wants to revolutionize the way the world communicates. With its cutting-edge technology and rapid expansion, it is powering the exchange of multimedia content around the globe, helping customers of every type and size to benefit from the full potential of the Internet. The company provides local communications services in 14 US states, specializing in broadband Internet data, wireless services, and video and voice communications with digital subscriber line. Its state of the art fiber optic network spans more than 104,000 miles in 14 countries. The company consists of two core businesses. One, communications services, provides Internet, multimedia, data and voice services to business consumer and government customers, including other data service and communications companies and Internet service providers. The second, construction services, builds and installs fiber optic systems for the company and other communications providers.

The challenge

To stay ahead in its vastly competitive arena, the company needed a top-notch, ongoing training program. The company's globally dispersed sales staff had to be continually updated in a number of functional areas, including the company's latest products, legacy systems, telephony-based systems and soft skills. Traditionally, the company had offered its workforce instructor-led and self-paced CD-ROM courses. However, there was no coherent means to track and document courses taken, monitor and access individual progress, or manage the registration process for classroom training.

They needed a learning management system that would not only provide accountability for the training function, but would also equip the sales force with skills to help them generate revenue faster. There were four immediate goals.

» Reduce training-related costs.
» Quickly increase the knowledge and skill levels of the sales force.
» Centralize the training function.
» Develop a competency program.

The solution

The company selected Docent to manage all of its training by creating a customized learning management system and e-learning portal. The system was fully Web-enabled, and provided a consistent user interface for the sales team.

The benefits

The introduction of the Docent learning management system has allowed the communications company to perform several new and beneficial operations, such as:

» the posting of classes more quickly than ever – generally under 10 minutes;
» the tracking of the training progress of individuals;
» the carrying out of online assessments;
» connecting with external training resources and systems; and
» registering employees for instructor-led training and create waiting lists.

Overall, however, the company's greatest benefit has been derived from the training-related cost savings, which will be 50 per cent for the first year alone.

The future

The company intends to expand the use of Docent throughout the company. More customized content will be created and third party content added. In addition, they will be taking advantage of Docent's Centra synchronous collaboration technology that will permit employees worldwide to enroll in real-time, interactive learning activities in a classroom-like setting.

A GLOBAL MANAGEMENT CONSULTANCY

One of the largest management consultancies in the world is reinventing itself to become the market maker, architect and builder of the new marketplace, bringing innovations to improve the way the world works and lives. More than 70,000 people in 46 countries deliver a wide range of specialized capabilities and solutions to clients across all industries. Under its strategy, the firm is building a network of businesses to meet the full range of client needs – consulting, technology, outsourcing, alliances and venture capital.

The challenge

To deliver the services its customers demand, the firm needs a highly trained and professional staff. The firm's emphasis on learning as a lifelong endeavor is taken seriously, and a significant amount is invested in training each year.

Even with such generous funding, it's a huge task. The company's shift from a few core businesses to many distributed businesses has resulted in an increase in the number of required skill and knowledge areas, which overlap organizational entities. In addition to training 10,000–14,000 new hires each year, the firm must also provide its existing people with the knowledge and products they require when consulting with clients. As a result, the thousands of offerings in the firm's training catalogue are in frequent flux. Moreover, because learning content has a shorter life cycle than ever before (content that used to last a decade now lasts a couple of years at most), this flux is increasing.

The solution

To meet the varied and ever increasing demands placed upon its training program, the firm chose to accelerate its move toward a unified, firm-wide, consumer-centric e-learning infrastructure. The company's goal was to have an intuitive, personalized, comprehensive information resource that would enable the firm's professionals to be even more effective information consumers.

Although the firm has no intention of eliminating its highly regarded classroom instruction program, it is transforming more of its training to a self-service, just-in-time function that lets professionals determine the training they need and when to take it. Their ultimate goal is to have a balanced program of 30 per cent classroom training and 70 per cent e-learning and other distributed forms of education.

The backbone of the new system is a learning portal, which aggregates everything dealing with learning into a customized portal that fronts the learning management system and provides links to other information as well. The firm chose the Docent Enterprise™ Learning Management Server to power this vital link. With Docent, the firm can offer not only traditional classroom training, but also asynchronous computer-based courses and live, synchronous learning events.

Benefits

Among the benefits, the firm has:

» integrated its own knowledge assets with those of external providers to great effect;
» streamlined the full end-to-end course management processes (registration, curriculum management, and reporting);
» was able to get the e-learning system up and running within three weeks;
» enhanced training access;
» improved capability building – entire teams are able to develop a common set of client-specific skills, yet spend more time with clients; and
» increased speed to market.

The future

The firm is now focusing on extending the use of the system by interfacing it with a number of other external systems, including their own HR and finance operations.

A VIEW FROM A COACH

James McColl of the Leverage Organization has provided the following vignette that describes his perspective on lifelong learning and how he has coached a senior executive to embrace the concept.

"Life has changed forever. Whether it is for the better or worse is a matter of personal perspective. However, one thing is for sure, we should now be playing to new rules. The smart people among us are aware of the changed conditions and are already behaving accordingly."

"Let's examine some ways in which life has changed. Well firstly, there are no more jobs for life. You probably heard when you were young, 'get qualified in this or that, or go and work for so-and-so and you'll have a job forever.' Is that the case today? I don't think so. Job security and loyalty (in both directions) is a thing of the past. We are only as good as our last performance. It's not just our peers that are 'snapping at our heels,' this is the age of globalization, mass markets and hence, competition from all quarters. The Internet means that we have access to ideas, people, organizations, and markets and thus opportunities and solutions to problems from all over the world. To survive, we must learn to deal with challenge, ambiguity and continually reinvent ourselves. Will change go away? No, not for most of us! It can be fun, but at first, for some at least, it may be scary."

"This ambiguity doesn't mean that we cannot plan. Far from it, the most successful people have a life plan defined in terms of goals, ambitions and achievements but the route we take may change by the day if necessary. Also, I do not mean to imply that we should stop qualifying academically and professionally. All learning is valuable. I just mean that our working lives should now embrace different disciplines and career opportunities. If we stand still, someone with a little more knowledge and skill will eagerly pass us by. 'It's nothing personal!' says the other person. Of course it was, he was thinking of himself. He saw the opportunity and grasped it. I do not mean to imply that we should help to create (or nurture!) a society where life is a continual battle. I am one of the greatest proponents of team working. We must, however, take ownership of our lives and not rely upon someone else. The employer/employee relationship is now more about a 'contract' of what can we gain from and give to each other. The period of the relationship is now less likely to take you to pensionable age, however."

"Can we do it alone? Well possibly, if you're that focused and motivated. However, most of us have a great deal of (typically family) responsibility outside of our careers; the purpose of the career for many of us. The problem is that we have little enough time to unwind, let alone design a life strategy for ourselves – if we knew how to. On the subject of families, there is much more demand upon us to provide expensive 'toys.' Kids want mobile phones, computers, designer-wear and travel aspirations. Who has to pay for it? Yes, of course we must sometimes say 'no' but have you ever observed/experienced the peer-pressure of modern youth. Then there's the two (three?) cars, the ever-bigger house, etc. We live in a time of greed. This is all stress inducing by the way!"

"There is help available and it does mean continual (lifelong) learning. Lifelong learning does not necessarily mean that every spare minute is engaged in academic study. We learn something everyday and should recognise the 'gold nuggets' as they come before us. There are times when we need the help of experts who can help us to recognise those nuggets and give us new ones to help us survive and grow. There are people whose job it is to help others develop and learn to embrace the new business life. A great starting point is to understand what you value in life and where you want to end up. The concept of mentoring is not new. The idea of learning something else is not new. What is new, is the need for most of us to recognise that the solution to survival and growth is a combination of: not being afraid to try new things, recognising our strengths and weaknesses, gaining new and relevant knowledge, knowing what we should and should not do and trusting a third person to help us to co-ordinate these things and give us advice along the way. Stress relief will act as a catalyst to help make it all work. This philosophy can help all of us, but the higher one is in an organization, the greater the need to stay 'in control' of oneself and life in general. For an organization to thrive, so too must its executives. Our approach at Leverage Organization is to provide a tailored plan for individual executives that will help them to cope with and embrace change and stress in their workplace. This will address not just business but personal/family life too, because both affect the other.''

"We support the coaching style of personal development because it has proven to be far more beneficial to individuals. Coaching is non-threatening and engages the person in a powerful partnership that leads to the person becoming far more 'worldly' and able to deal with life's challenges.''

"It is now recognised that to be most effective in this changing world, leaders require the skills and ability to be successful in dealing with interpersonal challenges and to acquire an in-depth understanding of the evolving relationship between people and the workplace and what makes them tick. So why do top managers invest in coaching and what advantages does it have for organizations in competitive industries? Many executives have found that a coach can provide independent personal support to help them be more effective in their day-to-day interactions. Someone who can help them to build a bridge from their present state to transform or stretch their visions for the future and ensure that their actions are consistent with what they are committed to accomplish. It is about supporting their commitment to lifelong learning and to raise self-awareness in order to adapt their behaviour to become more effective and fulfilled. It is through coaching, rather than providing more information to manage that will expand their capacity to perform.''

"There is the question of cost and the return on investment of coaching and personal development. It is now widely acknowledged that the only sustainable competitive advantage lies in the knowledge, creativity and skill of the people in the organization; 'human capital.' This is where the real value of the company now lies. In fact, according to *Intellectual Capital* by Thomas Stewart, editor of Fortune magazine, 'the marginal value of investing in human capital is about three times greater than the value of investing in machinery.' It makes good financial sense, therefore, to invest in coaching. It is, after all, the key to achieving the 'learning organization' that so many companies desire to create.''

"It will be useful, at this point, to mention a case study of a top business leader who has and continues to benefit from lifelong learning and coaching. We will call him Andrew. Andrew is the major shareholder and chairman of a group of companies engaged in retail and associated education. His group of companies has grown from a small family business. Andrew is a visionary, in that he's smart enough to recognise the potential in developing other businesses that can feed additional business back into the first. Great stuff! The problem is that the group had become too dependent upon his presence. He could not even take a day's fishing without taking his mobile phone (For those of you who fish, you will know that it's all about escape and solitude!) Actually, he didn't let himself escape because he considered himself to be the only one who could make the decisions. People in the group, therefore, felt that they needed his advice and approval for all types of issues, big or small. He didn't mind the big – but the small were starting to depress him.''

"Andrew started thinking about retirement. The big problem was, that although he may have been able to financially, he believed that if he was removed from the group, it would falter after a while and like an orchestra that suddenly loses its conductor, it would miss a few notes and degrade into a cacophony within a short while afterwards. A little dramatic perhaps, but probably a self-fulfilling prophecy because his people were ready for him to go. They depended upon him too much.''

"The people, as individuals, were all very capable but between them they were not organized in a way that enabled them to become more self-managing. To cut a long story short, we helped them design and deliver a change programme that looked at enhancing team-skills, a getting 'square pegs into square holes,' process review and put in place a series of personal coaching plans to help key individuals 'grow' into their new roles, that gave them each more executive authority. Andrew himself received coaching. He had to be taught to let go and trust his people to start managing the business. Only through his personal growth of learning more skills to effectively delegate, and trust others to make decisions, was Andrew able to move on. He continues to receive coaching to help him with his new role. His instinct will still encourage him to 'interfere' but he now knows when and when not to make a well-judged intervention. Andrew was always hungry for new knowledge and it was not difficult to help him change. He continues with coaching as he gets closer to fully disengaging from the business. He insists, however, that his people continue to learn new skills and receive regular coaching and mentoring from himself and our people.''

A PERSONAL PERSPECTIVE

The following vignette reflects Jan Hennessey's journey of lifelong learning.

After completing her ''A'' level examinations, Jan became a state registered nurse and it was during the early part of her nursing career that she met her future husband, a doctor. After the birth of her second child, Jan registered for an Open University degree and took the next six years to complete it. At the end of the course, Jan had the opportunity to recruit medical staff for a United States consultancy, which was setting up a medical school in Saudi Arabia. Jan realized that, although well qualified on the medical front, she could benefit from gaining greater understanding of personnel management. To that end, she used her salary to fund an Institute of Personnel Development (IPD) qualification on a part-time basis over a two-year period.

On completing the qualification, Jan decided to build on this by pursuing a career in training and development. She wrote to several organizations in her search for an opportunity to do so, and was offered a position with the Anne Shaw Organization as personal assistant to Anne Shaw, a role which became one of supporting consultants in the firm with information on current issues relevant to their special areas of expertise. This was a great opportunity for her to further develop her knowledge. Jan was then given the opportunity to lead a Manpower Commission Services Program of career guidance and support for unemployed managers.

The Anne Shaw Organization also ran an extended project management course, and Jan was asked to contribute to this with the coaching support of one of the senior consultants. This significantly extended her understanding of commercial operational issues to complement her personnel management experience. At this time too, the concept of "self development" was attracting growing interest, and following market research, and with the significant help of a colleague, Jan designed and launched a self-development based program for women managers. It soon became obvious to sponsoring clients that the program was as applicable to men as women, and this led to the establishment of a program that is still run regularly on an open basis, and in a tailored in-house format for a wide range of organizations.

In 1988, the organization was offered for sale by the owners, and Jan was encouraged to buy it with her husband. It was renamed Anne Shaw Consultants to honor its past and signal a future culture of working partnership and mutual respect within the organization. Since then Jan's role has broadened to include organizational leadership and specialist consultancy that promotes the principles and practice of self-development.

Now a fellow of the CIPD and CIMC, Jan maintains continuing professional development, and over the last 10 years has added to this a growing experience of higher education governance through membership of Manchester University Court and several committees. She has been elected onto the university council and in association with this, is exploring strategies for change.

Reflecting on her career, Jan values the fact that she can trace a path of incremental development that has provided her with opportunities to put into practice the learning achieved. She acknowledges the part that luck has played in the chances with which she has been presented, but she also knows that "luck favors the prepared mind" – one that plans ahead but is also opportunistic. Lifelong learning must also accommodate loss; after the death of her husband she is learning to pursue different objectives for her future than those she formerly desired.

Personal values constitute the threads of continuity in evolving life situations. Jan feels privileged to have been able to honor and promote her own personal and professional values in so many aspects of her working and home life.

Key Concepts and Thinkers

Lifelong learning has many terms and concepts, which have increased with the advent of e-learning. This chapter covers the majority of them.

What follows is a glossary containing the key terms associated with lifelong learning as well as a more in-depth look at some of the key concepts and thinkers.

ACTION LEARNING

Action learning involves three elements.

» The introduction of relevant concepts, theories, models and tools.
» The use of problems and simulations to test out the new concepts.
» The inclusion of opportunities to evaluate progress, discuss findings and change tack if necessary.

Action learning is believed to overcome one of the main problems with traditional forms of learning, the time lag between being introduced to the concepts and their application. In action learning, opportunities to practice are part of the learning process.

AFTER ACTION REVIEW

The United States Army uses the after action review (AAR) as means of continuous learning and improvement. The AAR originated during the Vietnam War, where the soldiers in the field knew more than those at headquarters. The AAR allows people to learn immediately after an event, irrespective of whether it was a success or failure. The key thing is that it takes place immediately. Conducting an AAR usually takes between 20 and 30 minutes and should answer the following questions:

» What should have happened?
» What actually happened?
» What were the differences between what should have, and what actually happened?
» What lessons can be drawn from the experience and how can any strengths revealed be built upon, and any weaknesses reduced or eliminated?

According to Chris Collison and Geoff Parcell in their book *Learning to Fly*, the AAR is a great technique for group learning and especially applicable to project work.[1] In addition, the AAR should form the backbone of the daily learning log discussed in Chapter 10.

COMMUNITIES OF PRACTICE

The concept of a community of practice was introduced by Etienne Wegner in her book *Communities of Practice: Learning, Meaning and Identity*. Communities of practice are a key component in the workplace and are relevant to lifelong learning. A community of practice is defined by three components.

» Mutual engagement and relationships. The nature of work dictates that the majority of people are engaged in similar tasks or require mutual engagement from others to complete them. For example, the claims processing department within an insurance company can be considered to be a community of practice because everyone is involved with the end-to-end process of managing the claims. Successful communities of practice depend on well-developed interpersonal relationships that are sustained over a long period of time. Without this it can be difficult to establish consistent outcomes and develop the feedback loops required to foster learning.

» Joint enterprise. Mutual engagement requires a joint enterprise that brings people together. As such it depends on the ability of people to negotiate roles and assume responsibilities and accountabilities for getting the job done as part of a well-oiled machine. Communities of practice are part of a wider network of practices that form the corporation. As such they will have their own identity and history and work under constraints imposed by the wider corporation such as finance, technology and people.

» Shared repertoire. The third component is the development of a shared repertoire that is about how work gets done. This includes processes, jargon, routines, tools, stories, symbols and actions taken on a daily basis. In many respects it creates a micro culture within the corporation and in essence is "the way we do things round here."

Anyone new to a community of practice knows that it takes time to understand how things are done, where people sit within the hierarchy, how processes work and so on. In short, it requires them to learn. In addition, through mutual engagement, the community as a whole is continuously learning as it adjusts to incremental and stepwise change within their own and the wider network of communities in which they exist.

CORPORATE UNIVERSITY

A university created by a corporation to train and develop its staff in order to maintain an effective and productive workforce. Corporate universities have the advantage of being focused on corporate needs, rather than providing a general education, as with traditional universities. By 2010 corporate universities will outnumber traditional institutions (see Chapter 6).

CULTURAL INTELLIGENCE

The ability to understand and be sensitive to different cultures, be they national, organizational or functional. This skill is particularly important within multinational firms, and in an increasingly globalized world (see Chapter 5).

DAMN

According to John Brown and Paul Duguid, authors of *The Social Life of Information*, learning is often treated as information delivery, training, or teaching – essentially a supply-side issue – but learning is principally demand driven; people learn in response to a perceived need. When people cannot see the need for what is being taught they will ignore it or fail to assimilate it into their daily routine. However, when they have a need and the resources are available they will learn quickly and effectively.[2] The DAMN model of learning recognizes this. The acronym represents:

» *D*esire – we all naturally possess the desire to learn and left to our own devices we will pursue some form of learning;
» *A*bility – learning is not just about receiving information, but making sense of it. There is a need to put learning into action, rather than remaining a passive observer. According to Daphne Yuen Pan, lifelong learning requires the learner to develop an inquiring mind that will prompt them to question and search, as well as higher order process skills that will enable them to synthesize, evaluate, adapt and apply the knowledge they acquire;[3]
» *M*eans – a solid infrastructure needs to be in place for lifelong learning to occur. This depends on both governments and

corporations taking the lead and creating the necessary impetus and channels through which people can learn throughout their careers. The Internet is one of the best channels with which to reach a large audience, although it still needs plenty of development to make it world-class; and

» *Need* – the accelerated growth of information and the continuous change brought on by globalization and technological change should provide enough of a need. But the key driver for us as individuals is the desire to maintain our employability and skills.

E-LEARNING

The management and delivery of training, education and learning via electronic media, typically over the Internet or an organization's intranet.

THE THREE "E"S OF LIFELONG LEARNING

According to Eddy Knasel, John Meed and Anna Rossetti, authors of *Learn For Your Life*, learning is important for three principal reasons – economy, empowerment and enjoyment.

» Economy – individuals need to be excellent continuous learners if they are to remain employable throughout their careers. By the same token, organizations need to be good at learning if they are to remain viable. There is therefore an economic benefit to learning both at the personal and organizational level. For example, research from the United Kingdom's Learning and Skills Council found that those businesses that invested an extra £50 per week on training increased profits twice as fast as those that didn't.[4]

» Empowerment – learning unlocks an individual's full potential thereby allowing them to develop further capabilities and skills.

» Enjoyment – learning should be a fun and enjoyable process. If it is fun, people are more likely to want to learn more.

EMOTIONAL INTELLIGENCE

The rules of work are changing. The ability to get on is no longer framed by intelligence, training and expertise; it increasingly depends on how well we handle other people and ourselves. Emotional intelligence entered management thinking with the publication of Daniel Goleman's book, *Emotional Intelligence*, and his second volume, *Working with Emotional Intelligence*. In it, he argued that there is an increasing recognition that emotional intelligence skills are a vital component to the modern corporation. This is especially true because most organizations are now heavily dependent upon people rather than products. And because being successful within the knowledge economy depends upon how well people work together, it is vital to be able to control our emotions. Lifelong learning requires that we develop and hone these skills if we are to maintain our longevity within the workplace. There are five elements to being emotionally intelligent.

» Being self-aware. Essentially understanding how we tick, including understanding our weaknesses as well as strengths.
» Managing the effects of our emotions. This means considering how and when to apply our emotions rather than responding automatically.
» Maintaining motivation under a variety of different circumstances.
» Understanding the emotions of others. This means paying attention to how other people feel and being attuned to the subtle signals displayed by others as you interact with them.
» Managing relationships. This covers how relationships in their widest sense are managed and maintained.

INFORMATION LIFE CYCLE

Taking into account the rapid growth of data and information within corporations, information should be treated like any other organizational asset. This means assessing its benefits as well as its maintenance costs. This can be achieved through the adoption and institutionalization of an information life cycle – designed to harness information that is of benefit to the organization and retire that which is too costly to maintain or adds no intrinsic value to the execution of its business. The beauty of such a life cycle is that it allows an objective assessment of information's value and its relevance to learning to be appropriately maintained. The same concept should be applied to our own knowledge so that we can replace outdated knowledge for the new.

INTEGRATED LEARNING MANAGEMENT SYSTEM

A learning management system (ILS) that is fully integrated into the human resource function and IT infrastructure.

KNOWLEDGE

Knowledge[5] falls into four categories.

» Know-what, which refers to knowledge about facts.
» Know-why, which is associated with principles and laws in nature, the human mind and society.
» Know-how, which is associated with skills.
» Know-who, which is the social ability to co-operate and communicate with different types of people.

KNOWLEDGE OBJECTS

Knowledge objects are chunks of knowledge or instruction that contain small amounts of information. They can be considered to be at the atomic level of knowledge and can be reused and customized to meet the specific needs of the learner.

LEARNING ABOUT AND LEARNING TO BE

Jerome Bruner, professor of psychology at New York University makes the distinction between learning about and learning to be. Most people learn about things, whereas learning to be requires the knowledge gained to be put into practice.

LEARNING OBSTACLES

According to Peter Senge, we all suffer from the following learning obstacles:

» I am my position;
» the enemy is out there;
» the delusion of learning from experience; and
» we fail to see the long-cycle changes.

As lifelong learners we need to eliminate these disabilities before we can truly learn.

LEARNING LIFELINE

Eddy Knasel, John Meed and Anna Rossetti, authors of *Learn for Your Life*, describe the concept of the learning lifeline. They believe that in order to grasp both planned and incidental learning opportunities you need to look critically at your past, present and future learning. To do this requires: an analysis of past learning to understand what factors helped the learning process to succeed; and, an assessment of future learning needs based upon your career aspirations and the goals of the organization. Once complete, it is then possible to construct your immediate learning needs that will move you toward your future goals.

LEARNING MANAGEMENT SYSTEM

A learning management system (LMS) is a software application that consolidates access to, and management of, corporate learning environments over the Internet or corporate intranet. An LMS typically automates registration, course scheduling, and record keeping, as well as tracking student progress and maintaining their profiles. A good LMS supports synchronous and asynchronous learning and provides powerful content management software. Systems hosted by third parties are capable of supporting synchronous e-learning activities, integrating with existing enterprise resource planning systems, and can be fully customized to client need.

LEARNING CONTENT MANAGEMENT SYSTEM

Learning content management systems (LCMS) create, manage, maintain and track e-learning content. They allow content migration, content reuse, tailoring to individual learning needs, asynchronous collaborative learning and integration with LMS.

LEARNING SERVICE PROVIDER

A learning service provider (LSP) is an organization that provides learning services to corporate clients.

LIFELONG LEARNING

Lifelong learning is both an attitude and a discipline that extends beyond vocational and work-focused on-the-job training, and which encapsulates the soft-skills such as interpersonal communication, teamwork, emotional intelligence and problem solving. Lifelong learning is principally focused on maintaining longevity within one's working life, and is controlled by the individual, not the organization.

MENTORS

Many organizations are turning to mentoring as a means of supporting the development of their staff. The most effective form of mentoring is that which takes place outside of the line relationship, because it ensures objectivity and limits the potential conflicts of interest that could arise. Good mentors are able to suspend judgment, build rapport, co-develop development objectives and provide feedback. There are four types of mentor:[6]

» the directive and challenging coach who directs the learner throughout the learning process;
» the directive and nurturing guardian who acts as a role model and provider of advice;
» the nurturing and non-directive counselor who provides support during the learning process; and
» the challenging and non-directive network/facilitator who helps the individual take charge of their own learning.

THE NINE INTELLIGENCES

We are all capable of developing our skills and competencies across more than the single dimension of IQ. Howard Gardner of Harvard University has identified nine.

» Linguistic – the ability to pick up languages, and the spoken word.
» Mathematical – the ability to solve technical, mathematical and spatial problems.
» Visual – the ability to visualize and manipulate imagery of all kinds.
» Auditory – the ability to pick up sounds, and play music.

» Kinaesthetic – the ability to sense your own and others feelings.
» Interpersonal – the ability to develop relationships with other people.
» Intrapersonal – the ability to self manage and direct yourself in the pursuit of your goals.
» Naturalistic – the ability to exploit nature.
» Philosophical – the ability to assess the ethical and moral dimensions of an issue.

NEUROLINGUISTIC PROGRAMMING

Neurolinguistic programming (NLP) is a relatively new concept that was derived from research into the transference of therapy skills between counselors. The neuro (N) component of NLP states that our behavior stems from the way we experience the world around us through our five senses. It also relates to our physiological reactions to the things we sense. The linguistic (L) element of NLP relates to the language we use to order our thoughts and behavior, and the way we communicate with those around us. Finally, the programming (P) aspect refers to the way we, as individuals, choose to respond to the conditions around us.

There are two elements to NLP that are of particular relevance to lifelong learning. These are understanding and changing beliefs, and maintaining peak motivation and performance. The former is about updating our belief system in order to become more effective. As individuals we all have barriers to personal growth that are embedded in the way we view ourselves, our capabilities and abilities. NLP provides the basis for reframing ourselves to become more successful by focusing on our underlying belief system. NLP provides some tools with which to do this. These include modeling and visualizing success, re-framing failure as an opportunity to learn, and understanding and adjusting personal values.

The second element that is relevant to lifelong learning is maintaining peak motivation and performance. This relates to how individuals develop and maintain peak states by associating these with their physiology. This essentially means identifying physical feelings, body posture and mental images associated with success, achievement and high performance and replicating these time after time. More importantly, it also means recognizing the physiology associated with low performance and either avoiding it, or having recognized it, switching into a more positive, high performing state. This plays on the well known fact that the brain's ability to process information is far greater when a person is in a high performing state than when they are low performing or anxious. It also means that, when in a high performing state, an individual is more resourceful and more able to overcome significant obstacles.

OPEN LEARNING

Open learning is a flexible approach to learning that places the student in the driving seat. Rather than following a strict course of study, open learning may start any time and is open to all (that is, there are no entry requirements). Study can take place anywhere, with the content and its order decided by the student. Most importantly, the learner can study at his or her own pace. The United Kingdom's Open University was one of the first universities in the world to introduce the open learning approach to gaining tertiary level qualifications.

SINGLE AND DOUBLE LOOP LEARNING

Learning involves four simple steps: step one, plan to do something; step two, do it; step three, check the outcome, and step four, take some action in light of the feedback. This process is known as single loop learning and is fine for our personal lives. However, within the working context it is rare to receive such immediate feedback because organizations are very complex and it can take time for the feedback from a decision or action to come through. So, to combat this, we have to deliberately seek out feedback from those around us. This is known as double loop learning and typically involves using the feedback to adjust our mental models, and, where appropriate, using external processes, benchmarks and other data to assess the validity of the decision or action.

SYNCHRONOUS AND ASYNCHRONOUS LEARNING

Online learning can be either synchronous or asynchronous. The former involves real-time delivery, with tutor support. All students are logged in at the same time, and there is the opportunity to debate issues and raise questions during the lecture/discussion by raising "electronic hands." Courses can be delivered using a combination of live on-line broadcasts, audio and video conferencing, Internet telephony and two-way satellite broadcasts. The latter involves a delay between delivery and feedback and typically involves recorded (videotaped) lectures, use of CD-ROMs discussion groups and e-mail.

SYSTEMS THINKING

According to Peter Senge systems thinking is a discipline for seeing wholes. It is a framework for seeing interrelationships rather than things, for seeing patterns of change rather than static snapshots. It is a set of general principles spanning fields such as management, engineering, and the physical and social environments. It is also a set of specific tools and techniques. Systems thinking is particularly relevant today because of the complex nature of the world of work.

TACIT AND EXPLICIT KNOWLEDGE

Thomas Stewart in his book *Intellectual Capital* makes the distinction between tacit and explicit knowledge. Lots of knowledge is tacit, that is, unexpressed and held within our heads. Years and years of experience, training and learning add enormous amounts of tacit knowledge to our intellectual capital. This leads to automatic responses and the application of judgment and gut feel to what we do. The problem with tacit knowledge is that it can be very difficult to articulate and is rarely found in manuals. According to Thomas Stewart tacit knowledge can cause major problems. First it can be wrong, second it can be very difficult to change and third it can be impossible to communicate.

Explicit knowledge can be accessed, built upon and repackaged. It is the very stuff of consultancies for example. Explicit knowledge is distilled tacit knowledge and takes the form of rules, processes, and procedures, is built into products and services and can be passed from person to person in a consistent manner.

UNLEARNING

According to Charles Leadbeater, author of *Living on Thin Air*, the best companies are not necessarily those that are good at learning. In fact, the best are those that can unlearn. He goes on to state: "Creative companies are cannibals. Their ability to unlearn routines they have come to rely on is as important as their ability to devise new ones. To make room for innovation, old ideas, products and processes have to be cleared away." In the same vein, we too must be willing to discard those things that are preventing us from progressing – outdated skills, knowledge, attitudes and behaviors. But just like any organization, we find this very hard because such things have served us well and can be difficult to let go of. However, failure to let go can lead to our early exit from the workplace.

NOTES

1 Collison, C. & Parcell, G. (2001) *Learning to Fly: Practical Lessons From One of the World's Leading Knowledge Companies*. Capstone, Oxford. pp. 76–85.

2 Brown, J. & Duguid, P. (2000) *The Social Life of Information*. Harvard Business School Press, Boston MA, p. 136.

3 Yuen Pan, D. "Lifelong learning: the whole DAMN cycle – a Singapore perspective." www.apec-hurdit.org/lifelong-learning-book/pan.html.

4 *Management Consultancy*, May (2001), p. 5.

5 Lundvall, B-A. & Johnson, B. (1994) "The learning economy." *Journal of Industry Studies*, **Vol. 1**, No. 2, pp. 23–42, quoted in OECD (2001) *The Well-Being of Nations: The Role of Human and Social Capital*. Organisation for Economic Cooperation & Development, Paris. pp. 18–19.

6 Clutterbuck, D. (1998) "Learning alliances." Institute of Personnel and Development, London, quoted in Hale, R. (1999) "The dynamics of mentoring relationships: towards an understanding of how mentoring supports learning." *Continuing Professional Development*, Issue 3.

Resources

Little has been written about lifelong learning per se, and yet it covers a great raft of material. This chapter identifies the best resources in:
» books;
» learning providers;
» websites;
» coaching organizations; and
» magazines.

"The illiterate of the 21st century will not be those who cannot read and write, but those who cannot learn, unlearn and relearn"
Alvin Toffler, futurist.

There is a world of learning opportunities around us ... all we need to do to is to seek them out and use them. Here is some of the best of the growing numbers of books, and online learning providers and organizations which can help design, deliver and host learning solutions.

BOOKS

The following books cover a wide spectrum of topics and encapsulate the essence of what lifelong learning is all about. As far as possible, the books cover in much greater detail the key topics and concepts discussed within this resource. Ranging from how the brain works through specific lifelong learning topics such as emotional intelligence and Neuro Linguistic Programming, to e-learning and personal coaching, this set of books constitutes a basic resource for anyone interested in lifelong learning.

1 Ian Robertson, *Mind Sculpture - Your Brain's Untapped Potential*. Bantam Press.

This is an essential guide to how the brain functions, how we learn, and how we maintain and increase our intellectual abilities as we grow old. In particular, Chapter 3, Pumping Iron in the Mental Gym, and Chapter 7, Use It Or Lose It, are particularly relevant to those concerned about maintaining their mental flexibility and adaptability.

2 Joyce Martin, *Profiting From Multiple Intelligences in the Workplace*. Gower Publishing.

A practical guide to using the nine intelligences of Howard Gardner (see Chapter 6). The book contains a large number of self assessment exercises, and provides a superb basis for assessing your balance across the nine intelligences. This naturally feeds into the self-development plan mentioned in Chapter 10. In addition, the book includes sections on the intelligent hiring of personnel and how to put the nine intelligences to work within the organization.

3 Daniel Goleman, *Emotional Intelligence*, and, *Working with Emotional Intelligence*. Bloomsbury.

The first of the two books is an introduction to why emotional intelligence is important, and why, therefore, being able to control our emotions rather than being victims to them is an essential skill in today's society. This general text was followed by a detailed look at why emotional intelligence is now a big issue within the workplace and how blind spots within our emotional competence can limit both our potential and ultimately our careers. This second book is essentially a handbook for managing our emotions within the workplace; it describes two groups of competencies: those that relate to how we manage ourselves, and those that determine how we handle relationships with others.

4 Peter Senge, *The Fifth Discipline*, and *The Fifth Discipline Fieldbook*. Century Business.

These seminal books brought the concept of the learning organization into the realms of management thinking. And although focused on the learning organization, we know that a learning organization cannot exist without people who are constantly learning. The first book introduces the important concept of systems thinking, outlines the principal barriers to learning (see Chapter 6) and moves on to describe the core disciplines of the learning organization, including the importance of mental models, personal mastery, shared visions and team learning. Probably the most difficult concept to grasp is systems theory, the essential element to double loop learning (see Chapter 8). Ultimately the first book is the foundation to the second, which describes how the "fifth discipline" is put into practice. The fieldbook is just that, a guide to making the fifth discipline work. It is full of case studies of organizations that have put the fifth discipline to work and brings the first book alive. Well worth the read as it also shows examples of systems thinking in practice.

5 Thomas Stewart, *Intellectual Capital: The New Wealth of Organizations*. Currency-Doubleday.

If you need to understand why lifelong learning is important then read this book. Stewart traces the rise of the knowledge worker from one of organizational insignificance to one of dominance, and describes what organizations need to do to get the most out of them. The key chapter for those concerned about their careers in the knowledge economy is Chapter 12, Your Career in the Information Age.

6 Dorothy Leeds, *Smart Questions*. Berkley.

With much of our working day spent with other people, being able to work as a team to achieve personal and corporate goals requires us to ask the right sort of questions. This book establishes the basis for asking better questions by introducing the smart questioning technique. Not only does it describe the types of questions we should ask, but it also details how questions should be posed to different personality types. For example, pose direct questions to the "commander" and open-ended questions to "carers." The book includes self-assessment quizzes and provides plenty of advice on how to use the smart questioning technique in the wider business context (recruiting, motivating, negotiating, delegating and problem solving).

7 Eddy Knasel, John Meed and Anna Rossetti, *Learn for Your Life: A Blueprint for Continuous Learning*. Financial Times/Prentice Hall.

Assessing our learning needs and the best ways to learn requires some basic understanding of how we learn. This book is a solid resource for anyone interested in pursuing the lifelong learning ethos.

8 Laura Whitworth, Henry Kimsey-House and Paul Sandahl, *Co-Active Coaching: New Skills for Coaching People Toward Success in Work and Life*. Davies-Black Publishing.

Although aimed at practicing and would-be coaches, this book is perfect for the individual. Not only will it help you to understand the coaching dynamic, it will provide you with sufficient information to begin the coaching yourself, and choose an appropriate coach should you want one. The most relevant chapter to the lifelong learner is Chapter 8, which focuses on client fulfillment and includes a very useful model, "the wheel of life," that allows you to assess all areas of your life including growth (learning). The coach's toolkit at the end of the book contains a complete set of tools and forms that can be used individually and that ought to be used by your coach.

Ultimately, there is no substitute for going out and getting a coach yourself.

9 Alastair Rylatt, *Learning Unlimited: Transforming Learning in the Workplace*. Kogan Page.

Rylatt provides a valuable source of information on workplace learning. As well as covering some of the basic models of learning, the book discusses the issues that have to be addressed at board as well as at individual level before an effective (and lifelong) learning environment can be established. An essential resource for anyone with responsibility for introducing effective learning within the modern corporation.

10 Martyn Sloman, *The E-learning Revolution: From Propositions to Action*. Institute of Personnel and Development.

This book is principally focused on the implications of e-learning on the organization, the individual and training providers. There is plenty of useful and practical advice for anyone wishing to understand the ins and outs of e-learning. Sloman uses plenty of case study examples, which provide interesting insights into the issues associated with e-learning at all levels.

11 Jim Steele, Colin Hiles, Martin Coburn, *Breakthrough to Peak Performance*. The Catalyst Group.

A very accessible and practical introduction to neurolinguistic programming, with a focus on achieving personal mastery. An ideal read before working on the self-development plan discussed in Chapter 10. Another useful resource on neurolinguistic programming is Joseph O'Conner and John Seymour's book *Introducing NLP* published by Thorsons. This book is particularly good as it describes how neurolinguistic programming can be used to understand and influence people, and is thus more externally focused than *Breakthrough to Peak Performance*.

12 Etienne Wenger, *Communities of Practice: Learning, Meaning and Identity*, Cambridge University Press.

The basic tenet of this book is that the learning process we go through (school, university, training programs at work and so on) are artificial, and fail to exploit the way we naturally learn. Because we all work, play and co-exist together, the learning process is much more socially oriented. This is especially true at work. Wenger offers an alternative model that is based upon communities of practice – that is the groups we work or play in which are defined by a common aim or interest (for example, the finance division or a fencing club). These communities of practice define the context of what we learn and because they are socially (i.e. people) based they depend heavily on the way in which we interact. Although quite a heavy read, it is a useful addition to the lifelong learner's bookshelf because it describes work-based learning. A second book by John Seely Brown and Paul Duguid, *The Social Life of Information*, published by Harvard Business School Press, offers a more accessible description of networks and communities of practice using Xerox engineers as an example (see Chapter 5, Learning and theory in practice, pp. 117–146).

WEBSITES/E-LEARNING PROVIDERS

Like anything on the Web, it can be very difficult to find sites that are relevant. The learning and e-learning market is fast becoming overcrowded with academic, private and not-for-profit organizations all offering learning solutions. The following sites are very useful, and interestingly, many offer a mix of electronic and classroom learning solutions for corporations as well as individuals. This is not surprising, as e-learning is unlikely to replace face to face forms for the foreseeable future (see statistics at the end of Chapter 4, for example).

1 Learning Matters (www.learningmatters.com)

Learning Matters is a virtual learning center that contains in excess of 1500 resources for the corporate and personal learner. The site offers a wealth of learning solutions including: training videos from Video Arts, self-development resources published by Echelon Learning, management articles and case studies from MCB University Press and Thomson Learning, e-based diagnostic and audit solutions from Echelon Learning and an international encyclopedia and management books from Thomson Learning. The site is well organized, up-to-date, and for the self-directed learner reasonably priced. The Virtual Learning Center offers just-in-time training suitable for a wide range of learning styles. The resource can be accessed via the Web, or can be hosted on an organization's intranet.

2 BlueU (www.blueu.com)

BlueU was formed in 1999 with the purpose of being the United Kingdom's first full service provider of e-learning. BlueU creates integrated, enterprise e-learning solutions. It provides a range of services that cover the complete life cycle of developing and delivering learning solutions.

3 KnowledgePool (www.knowledgepool.com)

KnowledgePool, recently named UK training company of the year by a computing magazine, offers IT and business skills training to corporate customers, government agencies and individuals via the Web and more traditional means. Online mentors located in the UK, USA and Singapore support the e-learning service. Students have access to online tutoring and mentoring, downloadable training material and real-time chat rooms.

4 CognitiveArts (www.cognitivearts.com).

An organization grounded in in-depth learning research. Its approach is focused on learning by doing (see entry on action research in Chapter 8), and goal based learning which aims to place learning within the organization's and individual's context thereby meeting genuine learning needs and accelerating the process.

5 Learn University (www.learnu.com).

Learn University is an end-to-end enterprise level learning service provider (LSP) offering comprehensive e-learning solutions to corporate clients. It offers a variety of distance learning programs and management tools to support e-learning. Learn University provides a one-stop shop for e-learning that includes:

» consulting services that guide the client through the e-learning products and services available and help to define learning needs and suitable solutions;
» course development;
» media conversion – modifying existing training material for use in a live (synchronous) and self-paced (asynchronous) environment;
» developing simple and complex assessment mechanisms;
» hosting e-learning environments using their network of worldwide data centers; and

> » offering a variety of learning management systems (direct or hosted through an Application Service Provider solution).

6 Noon Time University (www.noontimeu.com).

Noontime University offers educational courses for busy professionals who can't get away from work. This innovative site offers some 40, three hour, high impact, tailored courses covering management, administration and more general subjects over lunch periods and early evening. This addresses the common complaint that it can be very difficult to fit in longer training courses in a busy work schedule.

7 Maris (www.maris.com)

Maris is a leading electronic publishing and e-learning development company. Maris has developed Edugen, an XML based e-learning engine that creates and delivers dynamically generated web and computer based training for educational, corporate and public sector organizations.

8 Smartforce (www.smartforce.com)

Smartforce (formerly CBT Systems) has been deploying e-learning solutions for many years. They provide a one-stop shop combination of technology content and services related to e-learning solutions.

LEARNING MANAGEMENT SYSTEM VENDORS

The following vendors provide, build and host learning management systems. The list is by no means exhaustive, but is a useful starting point for anyone needing to assess the market. As most provide similar services, detailed descriptions of the sites and services have been omitted.

> » Docent (www.docent.com)
> » ISOPIA Interactive (www.isopia.com)
> » KnowledgePlanet.com (www.knowledgeplanet.com)
> » Learnframe (www.learnframe.com)
> » Pathlore (www.pathlore.com)
> » Saba (www.saba.com)
> » THINQ (www.thinq.com)
> » NETg (www.netg.com)

COACHING ORGANIZATIONS

Because coaching is an important element within lifelong learning, a small number of coaching organizations have been included. Ultimately, the use of a coach is a personal matter and it is important to select one that is right for you.

1 Speakers International Corporate Development (www.speakers-international.com)

Speakers is dedicated to making a difference in the world of corporate development, and is a strong advocate of lifelong learning. It believes that the most effective way of acquiring and applying knowledge is not only to create an interest but to deliver the information in a way that incorporates all the senses – audio, visual and kinaesthetic (see Chapter 8 and the entry on NLP, and Chapter 6). Its core program – Peak Performance – is must-attend, as it covers the essential learning tools and techniques we all need in the world of business, vital when conducting a stock take (see Chapter 10).

2 The Leverage Organization (www.leverageorganization.com)

The Leverage Organization offers considerable expertise in personal development and coaching – interacting with senior executives helps develop the organization as leaders. Its knowledge of human behavior and business provides a framework for supporting and advising leaders to adapt to the demands presented by new levels of change, the evolving expectations of the people they lead and the customers they serve. In partnership with each leader, the Leverage Organization explores potential new perspectives for dealing with current issues, thus inventing creative solutions to those issues that sometimes seem insoluble. This transformation entails raising self-awareness and altering the underlying context of beliefs and assumptions that shape, limit and define the way people think and act. Every relationship is unique and the approach taken is decided jointly by the individual and the coach. As a result of the professional support provided, business leaders find themselves better able to deal with difficult situations. Many believe that being effective with people and communicating well are two of the greatest challenges they face, and consequently can be the most difficult to successfully address. Through coaching, they enhance their capacity to have impact and influence in their organizations and find fulfillment in their lives.

3 The Coaches Portal (www.coachesportal.com)

This site is well worth a visit for anyone interested in finding a coach. It is operated by co-active coaches (see book entry eight for details) and provides a long list of coaching organizations mainly in the United States. There are one or two entries for the United Kingdom.

4 Anne Shaw Consultants (www.anneshaw.com)

Anne Shaw Consultants specializes in helping individuals develop their potential. One of the principal ways in which they do this is through a self-development program for managers. This is a modular nine-day program with the following rationale: "Self development involves people in taking responsibility for their own learning. This approach is driven by corporate and individual needs for effectiveness and efficiency. The program provides the framework within which managers can learn, in a practical and supported way, and teaches them how to take responsibility and turn it to their advantage and that of their organization."

The program comprises four themed workshops interspersed by periods back at work when theory is put into practice through individual self-development initiatives, and it is supported by a mentor who acts as a sounding board for issues and concerns, as they arise.

Workshop 1 – planning self-development. This covers the following topics: attributes of management; self-management; biography work; learning styles; and personal construct theory and transactional analysis.

Workshop 2 – the context of self-development. This discusses organizational culture; listening; politics and political behavior; management styles; assertiveness; and perception and feedback.

Workshop 3 – pursuing self-development. This addresses: creativity; resolving conflict; forcefield analysis; and team roles and influencing styles.

Workshop 4 – taking self-development forward. This focuses on two elements: counseling and networking.

At the end of the program, the individual has a better awareness of themselves and the ways in which to develop their ability. The introduction of theories and practical guidelines enhances knowledge about self-development and realizing potential.

MAGAZINES

1 *E-learning Magazine* (www.elearningmag.com)

A magazine dedicated to the whole topic of e-learning. The magazine typically covers a wide range of topics including technology, content and services. It is particularly useful for keeping up with the latest trends and concepts.

2 *People Performance Magazine* (www.peopleperformancemagazine.com)

As the title suggests, this is a general magazine covering the major human resources and career related issues of today. The magazine has regular articles on the topic of e-learning, and is a useful source of up to date thinking on the subject.

3 *Line Zine* (www.linezone.com)

Line Zine is a quarterly magazine introducing thought leadership about learning, performance and knowledge in the new economy. The e-magazine has regular interviews with the key thinkers on the subject of learning, articles on subjects ranging from measuring the return on learning to how to win the talent wars, book reviews, and a rich links page providing links to useful websites, magazines, articles and talks.

4 *Online Learning* (www.itrain.com)

A similar magazine to e-learning covering current topics in the e-learning zone, including content management systems, take up of e-learning, and so on. In addition, it provides a search capability to find detailed information on suppliers of IT training products and services. The paper-based magazine is available free in the United States and Canada.

5 *Corporate University Review* (www.traininguniversity.com)

Dedicated to corporate university practitioners around the globe.

Ten Steps to Making Lifelong Learning Work

Being successful at lifelong learning means:

» reading;
» asking smart questions;
» maintaining a learning log;
» creating a self-development plan;
» getting involved with projects;
» learning from success and failure;
» sharing knowledge;
» getting yourself a personal coach/mentor;
» getting yourself published; and
» undertaking regular stock takes.

"Learning is not compulsory . . . neither is survival."
W. Edwards Deming, quality guru.

"Learning skills, that is the willingness or motivation to learn, are critical to the success of tomorrow's employees. Candidates who have these skills will grow and learn with changes as they happen. As the job changes, these employees will be challenged to learn and master those changes. In the process, they will ensure their own success and the success of the organization."
Alan Downs, management consultant.

Because lifelong learning is down to you and no one else, the way to make it work involves taking deliberate steps to improve your own capabilities. This may require a major shift in attitude, but it will be worth it because it makes you more employable and in uncertain times this is precisely what is needed. The following ten steps will start the journey of lifelong learning and to be successful, they must be continued. Ultimately, however, it is about being opportunistic and seizing every learning opportunity with both arms.

1. READ

There is no doubt that reading is a great way to enhance learning and intellectual capital. What is worrying perhaps is that most people confine their reading to novels, newspapers and popular magazines. And, even when business executives pick up business books it is rare for them to finish them; they so often get bored or side-tracked. Too many books lie on the shelf gathering dust. It might look impressive to your colleagues and customers, but an unread book will add no personal value at all and ultimately any value to the organization as a whole. Therefore one of most obvious and easy ways to succeed at lifelong learning is to read and read widely.

Reading widely provides two distinct advantages. First it allows you to learn from the concepts, ideas, research and experience of others, which saves you time having to learn it from your own experience. Second it trains your mind to learn and connect varying concepts together – it is an essential feed into lateral thinking. It also trains your mind to accept new ideas more readily and makes you more flexible in your thinking. When most of your colleagues don't read, the fact that you do provides a significant competitive advantage in the workplace.

2. ASK SMART QUESTIONS

We are all guilty of asking too few questions, and yet we all love to answer them. It is a sad fact that we often pay more attention to someone asking questions than someone delivering the answers. According to Dorothy Leeds, author of *Smart Question*, knowing when to ask smart questions gives you the edge in any situation. In particular she believes questions: help to persuade people; gain information; plant your ideas into other people's minds; clear up thinking; motivate employees; solve problems; open communication between warring functions; overcome objections; get co-operation and reduce risks.

In many instances we fail to ask questions at all, even our most burning ones. And, once the instant has passed it is often very difficult to ask, for fear of appearing stupid. We should all take our lead from Lieutenant Colombo who asked so many simple questions that he appeared a simpleton to his quarry, but he was always able to solve the crime and get his man. Also Rudyard Kipling's six honest men

> "I keep six honest serving men (they taught me all I knew);
> Their names are What and Why and When and How and Where and Who..."

provides the basis for asking smart questions. Einstein never stopped asking questions, nor should we, it's a great source of learning.

3. MAINTAIN A LEARNING LOG

This is a great way to reflect on what you have done without the need to discuss it with other people. Although, if you have a life coach/mentor (see step eight) it is worth sharing the contents of the log with them as they will be able to provide you with some objective feedback. The purpose of the log is to develop the routine of self-reflection and analysis. Rather like a scientist who keeps a log of their experiment in order to assess the effectiveness of their approach, a learning log allows you to assess the effectiveness of your actions and decisions at work.

The log is very simple in so far as it should summarize what went well, what went badly, what you have learnt from the experience (both good and bad), and most importantly, what you might do next time to improve on the outcome. There are two questions you should ask yourself.

» What went well? When answering this question consider what you learnt from it, and how you can build on it.
» What went badly? Always a difficult question to answer, but essential to learning. When considering this question, identify why it occurred, what you can learn from it, how you can fix it, and how you can improve upon it next time. The use of after action reviews might help (see Chapter 8).

Keeping a learning log requires discipline, but there are significant dividends to be had, including the ability to identify areas that require improvement (which can feed into your self-development plan – see step five). Your learning log should be updated regularly and discussed with your coach/mentor (see step eight) and is an essential input into your stock takes (see step ten).

4. CREATE A SELF-DEVELOPMENT PLAN

A study during the 1960s found that those people who wrote down their goals were significantly more successful than those that didn't. Needless to say, very few did. We all tend to create some kind of development plan as part of our annual objective setting process at work. This is rarely as effective as it should be because we never fully buy into the process, as we see it as a means to an end rather than something that is personally beneficial.

Far better to create a personal development plan that covers the areas of our career and personal life that can benefit from learning. If you undertake to follow all of the ten steps outlined here, you can feed the outcome from your regular stock takes into your plan, share it with your coach/mentor, who should provide some objective challenge, and who knows, this might even help with your annual objective setting process. The development plan should begin by setting out your goals – where you want to be and what you want to achieve over the next three to five years. Then you will need to make an honest assessment of where you are now in relation to each of the goals you identified in the previous step. The next step is to determine the gaps between where you are now and where you want to be. And, finally you will need to establish what has to be done to eliminate the gaps and ultimately achieve your objectives.

When considering the specific gaps, it is likely that their elimination will require changes at work, adjustments to your attitudes, and behaviors, and seeking new knowledge through project experience or formal courses for example.

5. GET INVOLVED WITH PROJECTS

What separates the mediocre from the star performers is not their position in the organization, but the complexity and value of the projects they work on.[1] In the modern corporation, titles matter little. Far more important is the ability to demonstrate capability and build on experience. And, for those who want to enhance their skills and capabilities, one of the most effective means is through projects.

Projects, and increasingly programs, provide the ideal opportunity to assimilate new skills, gain a better understanding of the inner workings of the organization and develop the skills of an innovator. Pinto and Slevin, authors of *Successful Project Managers*, believe projects to be the engines of growth for the modern corporation. Because projects are about changing the status quo, those that get involved with them gain invaluable experience of their organization, change management and innovation. Moreover, because projects cause turbulence, it provides the training ground for the vital skills of influencing, politicking and stakeholder management. As organizations reinvent themselves over and over, they become more reliant on project management skills to do so. If you develop these skills you will be in high demand.

Interestingly, some companies, such as Ford Motor Company, are actually using projects as a tool for learning. They are combining projects with e-learning so that their high potential middle managers around the globe can fundamentally reinvent the way they work.

6. LEARN FROM SUCCESS AND MISTAKES (YOURS AND OTHER PEOPLES)

"Clever people learn from others' mistakes. Fools learn from their own." This quote from the Russian politician Alexander Lebed is perhaps a little unfair, as we all make mistakes from time to time. However, it is essential that we learn from them. More important is being able to learn from other people's mistakes.

Equally critical is the ability to learn from yours and other people's success. It is rare for people to reflect on either success or failure, and yet there are always insights to be had and lessons to be learnt. There are a number of ways we can learn from success and failure. For example, the UK's National Audit Office publishes reports on failed projects, neurolinguistic programming provides the basis for modeling other people's success, and the use of after action reviews allow us to reflect on recent actions and decisions (see Chapter 8).

7. SHARE KNOWLEDGE

In general we all tend to hold onto the traditional view of protecting those things that have scarcity value. In the past finding something out usually took time, effort and in some cases money. And because of this, it was felt the outcome of this activity was a personal possession. However, in the modern workplace, with so much information flying around the organization, this type of mindset is outdated and counter productive. Yet, we hear time and time again that people withhold knowledge that can be used to advance their careers or maintain their position in their organization.

The paradox in the information age is that sharing knowledge is power, rather than the other way around. Sharing knowledge need not be so traumatic, as, when we consider the degree to which most of our knowledge is tacit rather than explicit (see Chapter 8), it would be impossible for someone else to know exactly what we know.

Sharing knowledge has a number of benefits. First re-articulating what you know actually reinforces your knowledge and keeps it current because it usually requires you to revisit it. Second, other people can add to your knowledge and understanding by offering further insights and ideas, thereby increasing your own understanding. And third, if you are willing to share what you know with other people they are more likely to reciprocate. Ultimately, sharing knowledge is a collective process, where everyone in an organization is willing to take part. As a result we all collectively learn and the organization benefits. The key advice is to share your knowledge as widely as possible, maintain a network of knowledge sources and you will learn plenty in return.

8. GET A PERSONAL COACH/MENTOR

Coaching is increasingly an attractive proposition for busy executives and many organizations now take the trouble to provide mentoring and coaching for their staff. There is a distinction between coaching and mentoring. Whereas the former is much more active with the coach working through issues with the executive, the latter is more like a sounding board. Second, coaches do not usually have a deep technical knowledge of what you do, they are there to coach not teach. Their role is to bring out the best from you and to explore ideas with you without the critical eye of the technical expert.

Mentors are generally knowledgeable about your role/profession and can give more technical feedback and support. Although organizations provide mentoring for their staff, this is typically work focused and does not explore anything that is not work related. The purpose of mentoring within the confines of an organization is to provide some career guidance for those being mentored. Unfortunately, the individual being mentored is always half concerned with confidentiality and is often unwilling to share all of their concerns with their mentor. The advantages of external coaches is that they can be truly objective and the person being coached has the opportunity to really open up.

9. GET YOURSELF PUBLISHED

This may seem a bit odd, but it has some distinct advantages. Firstly, writing articles, papers and books requires research. The process of research forces you to learn more about the subject you are writing about and therefore increases your personal knowledge and intellectual capital. In addition, it begins to open up your lateral thinking skills as you draw the material for the article or book together. It fits well with step one, above, as research requires a lot of reading.

It can also be added into your self-development plan. Secondly, it increases your profile both within your own organization, and, more importantly, within the wider marketplace; both of which are essential to your longevity in the world of work. The third advantage to writing is that it allows you to reflect the material onto your daily work. This can be extremely valuable because it leads to new insights and ideas that may never have materialized had you not put pen to paper.

10. UNDERTAKE REGULAR STOCK TAKES

We can all get comfortable with what we know and what we do. Being competent is of course essential, but being good at what is needed today does not prepare us for tomorrow. Thomas Stewart in his book, *Intellectual Capital*, provides some key questions for us when we undertake our stock take and if we answer them honestly we will get a clear indication of where we stand in relation to our value to the organization for which we work, and ultimately where we stand in terms of our employability.

» Are you learning? When considering this question think about what you may have learnt over the past six months and what you expect to learn over the next six. If you are learning next to nothing it might be time to reconsider your position, as lack of learning may mean that your employer is not providing with the skills you (and the company) need for the future, or that you are not stretching yourself sufficiently to increase your abilities.

» If your job was advertised, would you get it? And similarly, if you lost your job tomorrow what would you do? Both questions are very instructive, as if you find it difficult to answer either then you need to consider what you need to do to ensure that you do. One of the best ways to keep ahead of the learning game is to read the appointments sections of quality newspapers. These outline the skills and attributes in demand and provide an excellent mechanism for benchmarking yourself against the job market. In these uncertain times you would do well to assess any differences between the skills and attributes employers are seeking and what you have and feed these into your self-development plan.

» Do you know what you contribute? If you don't know then does anyone else? Knowing the answer to this question will help you answer the previous one. It is not always easy to know how we contribute, but it ought to be possible to find out. Key things to consider here would be how what you do improves the bottom line either by delivering better customer service and sales, operational efficiencies and productivity gains. Knowing this and then considering what skills and attributes you use to achieve these outcomes will help you understand where your strengths lie.

The self-development plan should be used as the basis of the stock take, as should any changes in the market, your personal circumstances and so on because these may lead to a change in the objectives you established for the medium-term. This can change just like any strategy.

KEY LEARNING POINTS
Ten steps to making lifelong learning work

1 Read – as the majority of businessmen don't read, the fact that you do will yield real dividends.
2 Ask smart questions – asking questions, even those that seem simplistic will allow you push the boundaries of your knowledge.
3 Maintain a learning log – reflecting on what's gone well and what's gone badly allows you to learn from mistakes and build on successes.
4 Create a self-development plan – mapping out areas for improvement and learning and then following them ensures you continue to develop.
5 Get involved with projects – projects are a great way to collect experience and train yourself to develop new skills and apply them within different contexts.
6 Learn from success and mistakes (yours and other peoples) – if you can't learn from your own successes and mistakes, you can't expect to learn from others.

7 Share knowledge – keeping it to yourself is a sure way to limit your learning.

8 Get yourself a personal coach/mentor – it's worth having someone who can give you an objective opinion.

9 Get yourself published – being published is a great way to extend your knowledge and develop a wider reputation.

10 Undertake regular stock takes – just because you are well prepared for today, are you prepared for tomorrow?

NOTE

1. Stewart, T. (1997) *Intellectual Capital: The New Wealth of Nations*. Doubleday/Currency, New York, p. 206.

Frequently Asked Questions (FAQs)

Q1: What is lifelong learning?

A: See the Chapter 2 section: What lifelong learning is.

Q2: Why should I bother with lifelong learning?

A: See the Chapter 3 section: So why bother with lifelong learning?

Q3: Who is responsible for lifelong learning?

A: See the Chapter 2 section: The role of the organization; and the Chapter 6 section: Employers taking learning into their own hands – the rise of the corporate university.

Q4: I want to embrace lifelong learning, but how?

A: See the Chapter 2 section: Being successful at lifelong learning; also Chapter 10: Ten Steps to Making Lifelong Learning Work.

Q5: How can coaching and mentoring help

A: See the Chapter 7 section: A view from a coach.

Q6: What is a corporate university?

A: See the Chapter 6 section: Employers taking learning into their own hands – the rise of the corporate university.

Q7: What are the implications of the Internet on life-long learning?

A: See Chapter 4, The E-Dimension.

Q8: How have organizations and individuals succeeded at lifelong learning?

A: See Chapter 7, In Practice: Success Stories.

Q9: How do I find out more about the subject?

A: See Chapter 9, Resources.

Q10: What are the origins of lifelong learning?

A: See Chapter 3, The Evolution of Lifelong Learning.

Index

Printed and bound by CPI Group (UK) Ltd, Croydon, CR0 4YY

13/04/2025

14656564-0004